OUT OF DOORS IN DORSET

CRANBOURNE MANOR

Frontispiece

DEDICATION

To the man at the wheel—through whose care on roadways, narrow, steep and stony, numberless excursions into remotest Dorset have been made possible—this book is dedicated.

THE Author wishes to express her grateful thanks to Messrs. R. S. Crossley, of Accrington, the Directors of the *Observer and Times* for their kindness in allowing the reproduction of material contributed to the Nature column of that paper over a long series of years.

Her thanks are also tendered to Canon Sanctuary, of Sherborne for his kindly interest and encouragement, and to her son, Mr. R. T. Alston for his assistance in providing illustrations.

CONTENTS

FOREWORD

I HAVE had the pleasure of reading this book before its publication.

The Authoress, though not a native of our County, has been captured by its fascination, and has evidently explored it pretty thoroughly from end to end. With a practised hand—that of a trained observer and ardent lover of Nature—she has sketched with poetic appreciation some of its salient features and recalled some memories of its buried past.

Her careful first-hand studies of birds, insects, and flowers are lessons in observation. The chapters on Dorset poetry are well worth reading. I would call special attention to the review of Barnes's poetry in Chapter X, because it sets a high and true value on his poetic gifts, missing only one characteristic—his keen sense of humour. Wordsworth and Barnes were both, as Mary Oakden says, serious-minded men. But the former failed sometimes from a lack of humour, whereas Barnes possessed this saving faculty to the full, and his humorous poems are among the best, while they are also true to the character of Dorset folk.

I think this book should find a place on the shelves of every Dorset library.

C. LL. SANCTUARY.

PREFACE

A HETEROGENEOUS collection of chapters such as those which are to be found within the covers of this book might have been described as a series of studies on Dorset. But the writer has no desire to present them to the reader in terms of mental application, for their production has been the outcome of pure mental delight. The poet of Grasmere wrote that 'there is a pleasure in poetic pains,' and in the making of seemly prose there is pleasure in which is no alloy.

The aim of the book, if, indeed, it can be said to have an aim, is to quicken the spirit of observation in those who ponder over its pages, while attempting to present the natural Dorset with its long gone memories—as distinct from the human Dorset—in the charmed light of a belief that silver cups and saucers may even yet be found under the rainbow's ends. In cherishing that idea, the bigger towns of the County, with their long fingers stretching out into beautiful country, have been purposely avoided, for the ends of the rainbow do normally rest on green fields. The same reason must stand for the writer's omitting to mention the stirring times of the Monmouth rebellion, the Royal fugitive at Trent Manor House, the smugglers and their contraband, the rising of the Clubmen. These things can well be left in the hands of the serious historian.

As for the writer of this book, the urge is still upon her to follow fast in the wake of the rainbow.

MARY OAKDEN.

Chapter I

FALCON, TIERCEL AND OTHER BIRDS

THE peregrine falcons which have had their eyrie on the cliffs near Burton Bradstock for some years have now come further west to the beautiful yellow cliffs of West Bay. The far-reaching high-pitched 'kek-hek-hek' comes down to me from the sky as I walk on the beach under the cliffs. The yellow, sun-warmed cliffs perennially reflect the sunlight in the liquid green depths of the Channel, and to-day they throw back that half whimsical call to the ears as one walks on the narrow stretch of coast. At first one looks about for a craft, believing the sound to be a tintinnabulation from some motor-boat. But it is not so. No boat is on the water which, moment by moment, breaks noisily on the beach. Yet above the noise of the breaking waves comes the high-pitched call of the birds. A thousand feet up there hang in the sky, like spiders by threads of silk from a ceiling, two large dark birds. Falcon and tiercel are there, and even as one looks with binoculars well in hand, one of the birds drops like a stone to the cliff top. Some jackdaw or young rabbit has probably paid the penalty for a little too much publicity. Up the bird rises again, and this time I see the grey body and light-coloured breast as the half-whimsical, half-complaining cry once again beats back from the yellow cliffs. There is nothing weird in the tone. Not a touch of that peculiar call of the gulls which suggests illimitable space and time. For all his power of wing and mastery over the air the sea is not the falcon's home. But that motionless poise in the air is one of the splendid gestures of the bird world.

From the beach one goes by a footpath of comparatively easy gradient up to the cliff top through furze, where brown linnets and the black-cap live, over the wooden stile, and so gains a point two hundred feet above the beach. The falcon is again high over-head, poised some five hundred feet above the spot where jackdaws and starlings rear young on the dizzy edge of the cliff. With the aid of binoculars I see every movement of the bird, when, indeed, there is any movement. For the most part the falcon hangs immobile, a black spot in the upper air. Two sea gulls for a moment mob him as with a flip of the wings the bird rises another hundred feet and leaves the gulls below. There he hangs for five minutes—ten minutes—motionless until one's aching arms and straining eyes will bear no more. But the bird hangs on as still, apparently, as 'a painted ship upon a painted ocean.'

The wary pedestrian leaves the margin of the cliff untrodden, for there are V shaped crevices in the cliffs—chimneys I believe rock-climbers call them—which are merely bridged over by a platform of earth. These platforms are only detected from the beach. On the top one might suppose the ground to be solid. The long cracks in the soft turf are, however, a sufficient warning to the wise. Eight or ten feet of the margin of the cliff already visible, stepped towards the beach to be hurtled over in some future downfall, is, therefore a safe place for the falcon's eyrie. And here, sure enough, as we walk along just outside the area of the menacing cracks, are feathers beautifully soft, white and brown in colour, possibly off some wild duck's breast. A few of them are blood-stained. At this point the falcon has plucked her prey, for there also are grey feathers of a pigeon, and a few shining black ones dashed with bluish green which once belonged to a jackdaw. Shall we say that the falcons at the top of the yellow cliffs are helping to adjust the balance of nature ?

Out on the wild hill-tops many young birds must live an uncertain life. Some of them, when newly fledged, do not take wing so readily as mature birds do. Yet they move about unprotected save for the protection that numbers may give. When motoring in late July over the flinty roads on Giant's Hill—the straight Roman road of romantic history—I saw a flock of some twenty game chicks running along the rough road in front of the car. For some distance they ran on, and, as the car slowed down to avoid injury to them, took wing with one accord and disappeared over the high hedgerow, the rich chestnut backs and tails conspicuous in the sunshine. The fields on the top of Giant's Hill are very stony and rough, good for the growing of wheat, but probably deficient in the fine grit which these chicks want to help them in digestion. For this purpose they visit the partially unfenced roads.

After severe storms the Dorset shore may have a very melancholy tale to tell. I remember reading in an old book on Dorset birds, that in the winter of 1881-82 hundreds of razor-bills were cast up dead on the Chesil Beach. Guillemots suffered the same fate on the great pebble barrier. Even the stormy petrel, whose name leads one to imagine it quite at home in a storm, has before now perished in scores during severe south-west gales, the huge bank being littered with the bodies of the poor, driven creatures. Through the savage agency of winter storms the presence of many unsuspected sea birds, such as northern auks, has before now been detected in Dorset eighteen or twenty miles from the coast. One could add more to this melancholy table of species, but enough has been said to indicate the pandemonium of a severe south-west gale in the Channel. Let us now consider a more cheerful picture.

On the Chesil Beach. It is past seven on a beautiful summer's evening. Away in front the waters of the Channel, quiet almost as a pond, reflect the colours of a wonderful opal sky. To the right the sun is shining over Golden Cap some ten or twelve miles away, and as it shines it throws a long band of shimmering gold all along Lyme Bay. At the edge of the golden band the cruiser *Vindictive*, outside Port Bredy harbour, lies black and harmless upon the opal water. In front, and to the left, both sea and sky are of a most delicate colour, neither pink, nor white, nor yellow, nor blue, but all of these blended into an indescribable oneness, yet with less insistence than the tints of an oyster shell. Sermons in stones, did Shakespeare say? What then shall we call this?

At the edge of the water at the bottom of the sloping bank of pebbles, here some forty or fifty feet high, the fishermen begin to haul in the net or seine. A single tern flies overhead. The fishermen pull at the ropes, six of them at each end of the net. The two groups of men are a hundred yards or more apart, and they pass the rope from man to man. Six black-capped, swallow-winged terns, beautiful in their pearly-grey and white, patiently await the appearance of the net. The man who has climbed farthest up the bank with the end of the rope walks down and starts again at the bottom to pull with all his might. Each man goes down again in his turn. By and by the net begins to appear, and minute by minute the terns increase in numbers. Now fifty or sixty of them dart ceaselessly about in the air with the rapidity of swallows, and with much more excitement than a swallow could display. A cheap meal, they expect, is in store. Having powerful wings they live mostly in the air. They give a touch of bustling, striving life to an otherwise tranquil scene. The net is almost in. The excitement in the air is great. A few jelly-fish, having no solidity, drop incontinently through the meshes. Scraps of fish that have come up with the net are thrown to the excited terns, who catch them in mid-air. The terns, like other birds, are obsessed with the necessity of living. They must eat to live. Hence this confusion of noise and movement under an opal sky and over an opal sea. A little while and the terns depart as mysteriously as they came. Their nesting place is on the Chesil beach itself, where the bank raises its formidable barrier between the silvery waters of the Fleet and the sea.

* * * * *

The waterfowl which spend most of their time at the bend of the river have built a nest on the right bank among the reeds and rushes. Very quietly they go about their work up or down stream when no one is seen or heard, but if one inadvertently moves the bird will stop still in mid-stream or turn back to hide in the growth on the bank at the water's edge. It is so important that the site of the nest should be kept secret. Affecting concealment in a garage the play of nest-building is beautifully staged for me. These waterfowl swim with ease although the feet are not webbed. The birds have a frontal plate of sealing-wax red, and they bob their heads forward as they swim at a good speed, leaving a wake which spreads diagonally to either bank of the river. It is a sure token of a nest a-building when a bird comes down stream with the ends of a reed projecting from each side of its beak. Approaching the nest the bird's movements are very cautious. The pace slows down. One might suppose from the hesitation shown that the hen had forgotten the site of the nest. It is not so. The bird is making sure that no enemy is watching. The nest is on the opposite bank in front of the garage window, but waterfowl do not know that windows have eyes. Among last year's bleached reeds the bird deftly threads other reeds which are fresh and green. After a short outing on the placid river, up she climbs about her own height above the water where the reeds touch the grassy bank. No doubt the nest rests on the bank itself. Lined with fresh green blades of grass brought down stream like the reeds it is comfortable, and safe for the eggs. To-day the bird is sitting within her little house, and her beak moves from time to time as she weaves the bleached reeds more closely. Perhaps by now she suspects that windows may have eyes. The meadow in the hinterland of the nest is frequented by a ruminating cow. There is no danger from that source. But laughing children come to gather ladysmocks, Shakespeare's cuckoo-flowers, and the waterhen tumbles incontinently out of her nest and disappears under water. After a time she sedately returns and climbs up as before. It is the most interesting moment of the day's stagecraft save one. The exception is what may be described as the changing of the guard. One of the birds sails steadily downstream with or without a reed in its beak. On the water by the nest the bird halts and makes an audible, but quite untranslatable remark. The occupant of the nest at once slides down into the water and sails away, while the other bird climbs up into the house of reeds.

The new sea-wall and the esplanade at Port Bredy are once again free from holiday crowds. The prospect from the wall and the two old piers is exceedingly pleasant at all times, embracing miles of rocky coast on either hand.

On one side the yellow cliffs have many holes and crevices in which jackdaws and other birds live. One of these crevices is adorned almost from the top to the bottom of the cliff with the large cabbage-like leaves of sea-kale. In summer great clusters of the white kale flowers do further adorn that crevice. This plant does not appear again along many miles of coast. I like to think that the rock-pipits I saw to-day on the sea-wall live in the crevice near the sea-kale, that the young birds in spring may look out over the white rock flowers. To-day a long line of sea-weed, on the pebbles close under the sea-wall, marks the height of the last tide. Some, too, cast up by last night's storm lies on the broad, level top of the sea-wall. Both the higher and the lower level of the wall are alive with flies and other small creatures attracted by the sea-weed. That is the reason why the rock-pipits are on the sea-wall to-day. They run among the drowsy flies, picking them as they go for the small fry are there in hundreds. On no occasion have I seen such numbers of insects on the wall. They have survived the storm, but being exhausted are easily caught. Now and again the wind carries them along in little black drifts for a few inches until they find their feet again. The rock-pipits follow. If I advance too near, the birds fly to the wooden barriers of the

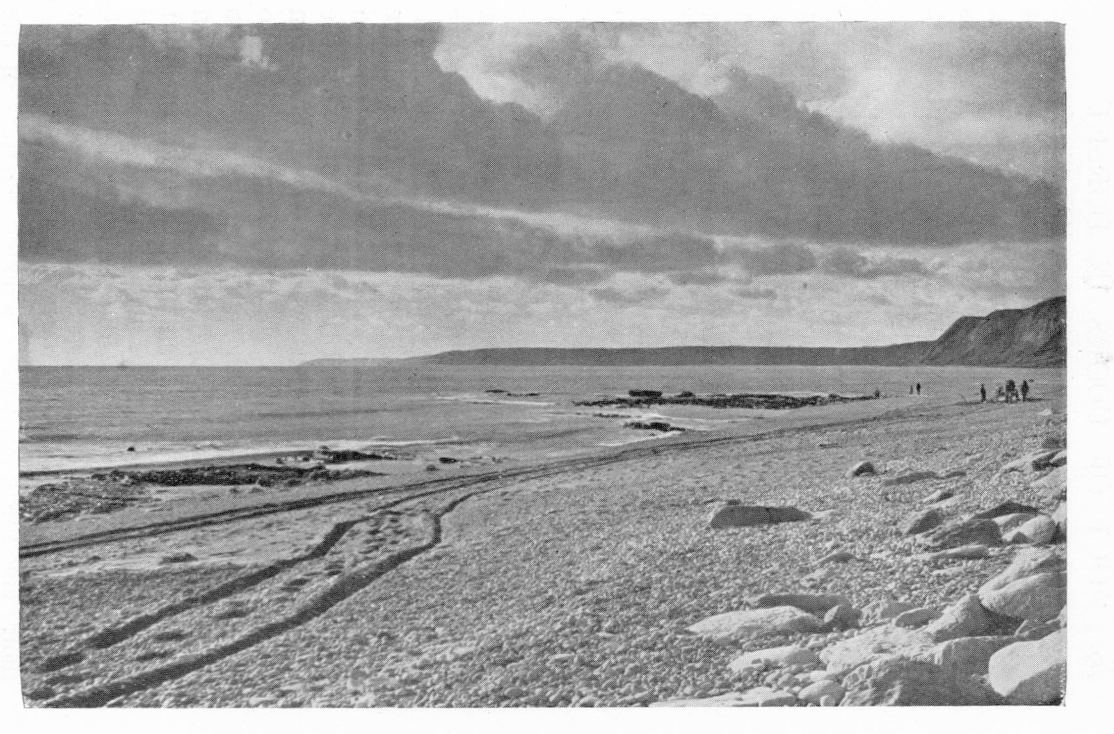

PORT BREDY BEACH AT LOW TIDE

harbour-way, between which and the old piers steamers come steadily to harbour with freight. The wooden barriers are overgrown with sea-weed below high-water mark, and the birds may there find flies as well as the small molluscs on which they also feed. While the new sea-wall was a-building, brown birds, larger than sparrows, were always about the men at work. Until I saw the brown birds to-day I was not able to gratify my curiosity as to what birds they really were.

The golden-crested wren, or goldcrest, the smallest of British birds, has a gold band running from the front to the back of the head. In winter, though so very small, goldcrests do not commonly visit houses as wrens and redbreasts do. Gilbert White contrasts the hardihood of these diminutive creatures with what he strangely describes as 'imbecility' in birds which migrate or seek food from the haunts of men. It is now known that some goldcrests do migrate even as other birds.

The goldcrest is a triumph of minute construction. Sir Walter Scott, impressed by its small size and its hardihood in wintering in England, wrote a sonnet to 'The Wren'—'Sonnet,' I said; well, the poem does not strictly adhere to the original Italian model of a sonnet, nor to the Wordsworthian type, nor the rhythm adopted by Shakespeare. But never mind that, Sir Walter's sonnet is addressed to the wren, and the goldcrest is often spoken of as the golden-crested wren. This little bird often builds its nest near the top of a high fir or pine tree, and that fact accounts for Sir Walter writing:

> Small as thou art thou gem-like bird,
> Yet thou hast built thy nest on high.

And again:

> Lovely bird ! with thy golden crown.

Now the common wren, Jenny wren, has not a golden crown, though deserving one, if only for the way the bird has of pouring out its heart in absolute abandon of song on the first sunny days of spring. The wren, too, is bigger than the goldcrest which, all told, scarcely measures three and a half inches in length. Like the wren, the goldcrest finds a contributor to its welfare in the spider world, for cobwebs are used in the making of the nest. Jenny wren feasts on spiders as a part of her winter fare.

Chapter II

BIRDS IN WINTER

The redwings in a recent year left the meadows under Bothenwood immediately after January 27. On that day I feasted my eyes upon their beautiful colours, knowing that ere long the birds would be flown. It was the last day of the frost. The next day the elm tree tops were shrouded in sea fog. The great soft white sheet drifted slowly inland and hung about hill, avenue, and woodland. Pressed close to the trunk of an elm tree to catch any sound that might come through the fog, I could hear the twittering of a vast concourse of birds. It was impossible to distinguish anything but the bare outline of the trees. Not a redwing was to be seen upon the ground. The birds had assembled in beech trees standing in the open meadows, on elms, limes, and sycamores banked together on the slope of the hill. Next day when the fog had gone the clearness revealed no redwings, though I swept the trees, the meadows, and the wood for half-an-hour with glasses.

A few fieldfares remained. These birds spend their time in the tree tops, and the hard 'tsak tsak' comes down frequently from the tall elms. They seem more nervous when the redwings have gone, but their manners are audacious compared with the first shy arrival of last autumn. This, a solitary bird, alighted near a small stream, and was promptly mobbed by a covey of local blackbirds which chattered loudly among the willows about the grey and slate-blue apparition. To escape this unwelcome attention the fieldfare flew to the elms of the avenue. The chatter of the blackbirds was very noisy indeed, and, though apparently menacing, was really quite harmless. When a green woodpecker and a brown wood owl come into collision on Bothenwood on a matter of some importance, then does the woodland ring with harsh laugh and vituperative screech. No covey of blackbirds could attain to any such demonstration. At such a time there is real war in the air, not a mere sensational chattering about the coming and the garb of a stranger.

Flocks of starlings are numerous at the moment in the neighbourhood of Port Bredy. In the meadows towards the sea they feed together with lapwings, gulls, and rooks. A little group of larks may sometimes be seen there. When the starlings are frightened they all rise at once with a rush of wings, and blacken the ground when they drop again. The larks, on the contrary, rise one by one when alarmed and go a little further away from the observer. One of them, it may be, runs behind a tussock of grass and goes on with its search for food. Molluscs, which look like minute snail shells, abound at times on blades of grass near the sea. I have seen a score of them on a square foot of grass. Food of some kind is abundant at the moment on which these flocks of birds of various kinds subsist.

On Stony Head a few days ago, when I went to look for redwings on higher ground—and did not find them—a flock of starlings came down from the blue overhead, and alighted in an adjacent field. Between me and the birds a deep cutting on the high road to Casterbridge intervened, and I was able to observe them unseen. They dropped in the pasture in the formation of a long curved line, like the top of a fan, and fell at once to steady feeding. I watched them for some time pushing forward, still in formation, clearing yard after yard of the pasture from some sort of pestilence. Yet few people have a good word to say for starlings. In one place where the birds were five or six deep, those at the back flew over the heads of those in front and alighted before them making a new front line, so jealous are they of others faring better than themselves. On the housetop the starling is an engaging humorist, imitating the call of all his feathered friends—of the thrush and even of the little owl. The call of the curlew from the throat of a starling I never hear in the South, as I often did in the North.

The cold days of early February are not without interest out-of-doors. The sky, it is true, is dull. A few mocking gleams of sunshine brighten the avenue now and again, but the light among the branches and twigs reveals no colour of any kind. Everything appears to be black—black twigs, black branches, black trunks. Both little birds and big birds appear of one uniform blackness against a grey sky. It is enough to make one petulant, for up there among the twigs and branches of the elms beauty is flitting about—ostentatiously flitting about in an avian paroxysm of pride. A family of long-tailed tits is taking the air at a great height among the finest elm twigs. There are about a dozen of them. I know by their ceaseless movements, their fluffy bodies, any one of which would go into an egg cup, and their long tails, that they can be nothing else. The thin little note 'ze-ze-ze-ze' comes down to me from the tree tops. But I want to see their colours. And even as my impatience grows, one little mite flies to the next tree, a twenty foot flight through the air, his long tail giving balance to his feather-weight of a body just as a stick gives poise to a soaring rocket.

Assuredly one dozen long-tails has survived that January spell of sharp frost. A little more patience and a bird comes low enough for the rose-pink of his feathers to show up in relief against the trunk, where the lichens are greyest and greenest. This bird is not blue like the tom-tit. It is rose-pink, and white and brown. The longtail is a dainty bird. And what place a cynic might ask do these elaborately coloured pigmies play in the scheme of things. Well, they destroy great numbers of infinitesimal coccids, larvæ, &c., found upon the bark of trees—scale insects so lowly that some of them possess no power of locomotion. These things abound among the lichens which cover the trees. The longtails do their share in keeping down such pests. To-day the severe spell of Arctic weather begins definitely to relax. Where, one wonders, are the tiny long-tails now? Did they roll themselves into a ball and retire within some sheltered hole as they are said to do, while the demon frost held the land?

'There are a lot of birds lying dead about the lanes and fields,' said a youth to me this morning.

'What sort of birds?' quoth I.

'Thrushes and little birds,' came the reply. 'I saw a dog chasing one thrush, it was very weak,' he said. 'I stopped the van and stoned the dog, and put the thrush into the hedge where the dog couldn't get it,' he continued, feeling obviously that he had only done what he ought to have done.

There is much promise in the midst of sadness for Nature-lovers if this youth is to be regarded as a representative of the sentiment of Young England to-day. A youth incapable of the usual cheerfulness because of the Arctic slaughter of wild birds is no novelty in the South of England. More was to come.

'Have you seen any birds lying dead about the lanes in your rounds?' I asked a fair-haired Saxon with whom I often talk about the birds and beasts of the district, when he calls on business.

'Yes,' came the laconic reply, given with an effort.

'What sort were they?' I questioned.

'Thrushes and blackbirds,' the youth responded,

and, for a minute, I found it necessary to make conversation while he recovered composure.

Such is a real love and sympathy for the helpless creatures of the field in a painful time of stress. From another youth I learned that thrushes and starlings were most numerous as casualties in his locality. 'More thrushes than starlings,' he explained. The heavy mortality among thrushes is in keeping with all findings of what has happened in severe frosts in the past. When the ground is hard the principal source of food for thrush and fieldfare is cut off, and the blackbird, who is very fond of water, suffers much from thirst.

During the spell of Arctic weather our pensioners throve and increased both in numbers and boldness. A blackbird and a redbreast sturdily came indoors. In view of this familiarity a wooden hut, where fuel is kept, was left with door ajar. Within was water to drink and bread to eat from morning until night. Instantly the improvised restaurant became popular. The blackbird led the way. A redbreast followed, and then a thrush. A second redbreast somehow got wind of events and boldly crossed the threshold. This, naturally, led to the expulsion of one robin by the other, but which one was expelled it is impossible to say. The two are as like as two peas. A grey-headed wagtail, apparently of Siberian type, also went inside day after day and partook leisurely of the feast. This bird has a way with him which is entirely his own. He is a traveller, and also, I think, a philosopher. His movements are deliberate, his attitude attentive, his mentality above the average. He is not suspicious. He will risk things just as a robin redbreast will. Robin is somewhat of a gambler. One day I chanced to go in the hut when he was there. He flew to the window. An impulse to possess him for the space of a few minutes took hold of me. In a twinkling he was caught. He did not peck. He made no sound. Under my lens I examined his eye—that wonderful black bead—and the orange feathers of his breast, the olive-green of his back. I stretched out one of his wings. He did not wince nor flutter. Then he was set free. Within fifteen minutes he was in the hut again, careless of risk of any kind. He comes many times a day. A blackbird was taken in the same way. He showed no fear while the brown irises and the orange rim round his eye were duly observed under a lens. When set free his excited chuckles as he flew away roused all the starlings in the neighbourhood to vocal applause. It was a great adventure. His confidence in the attendant human being is, however, no whit lessened.

The river Asker a few days ago was covered with ice. From my window I can see the sharp curve which the river describes under the willows as it comes round the bed of reeds where the water-hens live. Here, when the sluices lower down are closed, the water is very still, and the willows and poplars are reflected in the deep water. So, too, are the white sea-gulls as they swim or alight on the water, and, in alighting, look for all the world as if one was coming up from the bottom, and another down from the sky, until the moment when bird and reflection combine. About fifty yards below the curve the river makes another curve less abrupt than the one by the reed bed. When ice covered the river a few days ago there was a narrow ribbon of open water on the inner side of this curve, and a ledge of ice ran along the edge of the bank and made a platform on which the starlings alighted to drink. Groups of six or seven stood and drank together from the narrow ribbon of water. At first sight they appeared to be standing on the water itself. Apparently they enjoyed the novelty of the situation. Blackbirds and thrushes are not so resourceful. They drink from the bath of water placed for them in the garden. Tomtits and sparrows do the same, sipping the water as if it were nectar.

* * * * *

To-day the garden is deserted. There is a breath of spring in the air, and birds have gone to the fields. The cornstacks above the willow-lined stream, where fieldfares first appear in autumn, are alive with finches and buntings. A flock of birds flies from and out of the great yellow piles of threshed wheat as one approaches. They go to the willows by the brook thirty yards away down a gentle slope. Many of the willows have been cut and laid along to form a fence, and at first it is impossible to see the birds after they alight. Their colours harmonize so well with the chocolate of the ploughed field above and beyond the stream ; with the drab of bleached reed stalks, and the green of ivy and harts-tongue ferns ; with the russet and dull red of willow branches and dogwood that they are almost invisible. Let us wait until a bird moves, and then promptly adjust the glasses. A little way upstream goes one with a yellow head and reddish-brown wings—a yellow-hammer. Another follows and then another. They are stealing back to the stacks by a circuitous route. There is a redbreast perching on a willow branch watching us as we watch him. Another goes upstream, with more yellow-hammers. A hen chaffinch deftly preens the grey feathers of her breast waiting for the general move of her kind. But the chaffinches are in no hurry. Their grey and pinkish breasts dot the willow branches.

In the corner of the field where the hedge is thickest a wondrously beautiful greenfinch perches on a bramble stem. He is green as the leaves of fresh ivy, with a gallant splash of yellow on either wing. My companion gives vent to an exclamation at such beauty in a British hedge bird. A few feet away the hen greenfinch, with her breast of yellowish-grey, can also be seen, and near at hand are more of the yellow buntings. At the top of the slope beyond the stream many birds have their nests in summer in three tall blackthorn hedges which rise one above another. Each hedge is on the extreme edge of a terrace of ploughland, where three such terraces lie one above another as the hedges do. When in spring the blackthorn is covered with white flowers the scene is singularly beautiful, as seen from the narrow road running by the cornstacks. A badger lives there, his burrow or hole in one of the terraces. There, too, the long-drawn 'me-a-o-w' of some kind of owl may, on occasion, startle one on a late afternoon in February. Owls are often heard an hour or two before sundown.

After the hard weather of January and February, 1929, when even in Dorset severe frost caused many birds to die from hunger and thirst, redwings did not appear in the meadows under Bothenwood according to their wont. Last year none were seen. But now a small flock of the birds is with us again, sharing the meadows with the young spring lambs. The January sun is low, and slanting along the ground where the birds feed, touches up their bright chestnut wings and thighs to an almost crimson colour. The redwings stand upright in an attitude of alertness when they find themselves observed, and a deep 'puck, puck,' which seems to be half chuckle and half warning comes first from one and then another. Under the bare trees of the avenue of elms they are obviously full of the pure joy of living. Their chuckling seems to be a gesture of fun provoked by my curiosity. They do not know, as I look upon them admiring their sprightly forms, that I think of the peregrine falcon, which, anon, may soar aloft above the pines on the ridge of Bothenwood. Their lively forms, their beautiful colours, their intrepidity by land and sea on long migratory journeys will avail them nothing before the savage bird of prey.

In the hurricanes of December, 1929, and

January, 1930, the avenue of elms suffered grievous losses. Some nineteen trees near a century old fell before successive onslaughts of fierce winds. Long gaps have since been relieved by the planting of young trees, two for each one lost. At the entrance of the avenue a far-spreading wych elm stretches its beaded branches over the avenue roadway and over a narrow lane which runs off to the left. From my window I can watch its long arms 'beckoning to the woodland hoar.' So long are its branches that they almost touch the nearest trees of a small plantation of spruce firs, where a number of tiny goldcrests live. These little birds are diminutive, fluffy creatures that remind one of toys and would barely fill an egg-cup, feathers and all. They are greenish-brown with white bands on the wings, and buffish-white feathers beneath. Their tiny beaks seem small and sharp as a pin. The chief glory of the birds lies in the yellow band, a quarter of an inch wide, which runs over the top of the head like a crest. In giving the width of the crest as a quarter of an inch no allowance has been made for the magnifying power of the binoculars.

The name of goldcrest has nothing sentimental about it. The birds will hang wrong side up under a twig of spruce with all the abandon of a tomtit under or in a cocoanut, picking aphids from the narrow leaves of the spruce. Goldcrests are common in Dorset. One of their loveliest haunts is on the northern side of the race down which is the most westerly point of the Pilsdon range. The down gives its name to

Racedown, the massive square-fronted house where Dorothy and William Wordsworth lived for a period 'in the midst of woods as wild as fancy ever painted,' to use Dorothy's own description. Did she, one hundred and thirty-five years ago, know the goldcrests' haunt near Speckett's-lane, which runs its capricious course along the steep, northern side of the down ?

The narrow lane which runs off to the left under the spreading branches of the wych elm at the entrance of the avenue, follows its sequestered way to a small village a mile off. It is bordered on one side by cultivated fields, and on the other by narrow meadows which slope down to a babbling, bird-haunted brook. At this time of year yellow buntings and greenfinches are here in considerable numbers, for this is the season when the hardier migratory birds from northern regions live amongst us in comfort and plenty. I may count twenty of the buntings or yellow-hammers at a single glance. Few birds vary more in the amount of showy colour displayed than do one- and two-year-old yellow buntings. Some of the birds have yellow heads and necks. Others are marked with darker colours on the yellow, and some are striated in brown and green. These last are the hen birds. All are beautiful under close observation. A flock of twenty or thirty flying low in the sunshine is wonderful to behold, flashing green and gold in flight.

The meadows below the road being strewn with hay and straw for the sustenance of young cattle wintering in them, make splendid provision for the small army of green and yellow birds. A dozen canary-yellow gleams, paler than the buntings, which flash across the road in front, signify that so many dark-eyed greenfinches have taken alarm at our approach. The 'look-out' on the tree-top, with the oft-repeated 'dree, dree,' meddlesomely tells the flock of possible danger at hand. But one contented greenfinch is not to be intimidated. He stands boldly on the sheaves, remaining on the high pitched cart left horseless in the meadow, and goes on feeding only five yards away. No need for binoculars now. He pulls out a full ear of wheat and extracts the fat and fattening grain. What cares the bird for anything with an ear of precious wheat packed so full before him? Another plucky bird of a lighter shade of green—for greenfinches are not all of the same tint—eats his meal on the ground before us. This bird also is less nervous than the canary-yellow gleams which flashed across the roadway at the sound of the look-out's 'dree, dree.'

Chaffinches and yellow-hammers when alarmed fly in a cloud to the alders and willows which mark the course of the brook and disappear as if by magic among the purples, russets, browns and greens of ivy and harts-tongue fern, and the bark of pollard trees. Alder and willow alike have been cut and laid horizontally to form a boundary on the farther side of the stream, and hundreds of new straight shoots, like long fingers pointing upwards, stand bare in the winter sunlight. The birds do not alight on the long bare shoots, where their forms, though not colours, might easily be seen. The boughs which have been laid give to them the obscurity which they seek. Their colours and forms melt away in the hedgerow of the babbling brook.

On the upper side of the narrow lane where the fields rise rather steeply, the turnips are divided into sections about a couple of acres in extent, by wicker wattles or hurdles. Sheep and young lambs are confined in each section in turn, where they eat up both green crops and roots. A flock of wagtails, both white and pied, have fed for several weeks among the turnips and among the sheep. The white wagtails appear to be wintering in the district, and the pied are probably migrants travelling with the whites. The clean-cut black bib of the white wagtails is a very distinct feature.

The shepherd's dog is always on the alert to attend to his master's business. When two sheep charge each other and the clatter of their horns is heard, the dog bounds over the ground and separates them in a twinkling. Dorset sheep of both sexes have graceful curling horns, and the impact of horn upon horn sounds like combat with wooden staves. These sheep are a distinct breed. In the South of England where new lambs begin to arrive in October and continue to increase until March, the old English sheep-dog, as a part of the scheme of things, is most intelligent and valuable. He has a longer lineage than his Scottish compatriot, though his fame is not so much noised abroad. There is one side of his nature which is not apparent to every one. The old English sheep-dog is very affectionate. I have seen him kiss the shepherd, making the approved osculatory motions with his lips, while a soft, caressing look came into his dreamy eyes.

During stormy weather flocks of sea birds come to the meadows by the river, and when the morning sun in January glints over Bothenwood and lights up the low, wooded hills, and bathes the lichen-covered trunks of trees in a pinkish-helio light, then is the time to watch the sea birds rise. The low sun catches the white feathers as they ascend into the air and turns the flock into a cloud of silvery, wheeling figures against a background of trees or blue sky. The brightness of an aeroplane cannot compare with the silvern plumage of sea birds, for their feathers do not glint, or sparkle, but suffer a rapid sky-change into something rich and strange. A movement of the flock, as the birds adjust themselves to currents of air, turns the clouds of silver wheeling figures back again to white, to be silvered yet again in a moment's swift precision. One may see the feat performed a dozen times while they remain in sight. The birds do not sleep in the meadows though they are there at dawn. One rarely hears the call of a sea bird in the night. In high winds, both sea birds and flocks of rooks play at aerial games at a great height, and sometimes the white flock may be seen above the black one. A flock of starlings, at a lower level, will on occasion emulate the bigger birds. I have seen them in a quiet hour, fly in and out amongst themselves with evolutions comparable to those of swallows in grace of movement, though not in speed. For a moment I have been deceived.

When hard weather comes rooks visit a cluster of sombre holly-oaks which I see from my window. The holly or holm-oak is an evergreen, and considering its great size it bears very small acorns. On the tops of the tall trees the birds alight with much cawing and fluttering of wings, as the long twigs bend beneath their weight. Apparently they come to take toll of the acorns. When not ripe, these fit very tightly in their cups, which are deep in comparison with those of an English oak. The difficulty here encountered will, no doubt, explain the noisy ado which one hears when the birds make their visits. Obviously, there is much discussion about the best way to extract obdurate acorns from their tight little cups.

Lapwings may often be seen near sea birds and rooks in winter when flood water lies in the river meadows not far from the sea. They feed near the edge of the water in the fields. I have seen a company of a hundred in the meadows take wing altogether, their white and green winking bewitchingly in the sunshine. The flight of the green plover is singularly beautiful. The movement of many rounded wings lapping, as it were, against the sky, might be described as the poetry of motion, did it not seem more nearly allied to music than to verse. One day in autumn I saw a flock of many lapwings fly out over the Channel at a good height. I watched their progress until as faint specks in the sky they melted into the distant haze. That was a flock of migrants making, apparently, for the north-west coast of France.

Chapter III

THE CHESIL BANK AND THE FLEET

The greatest volume of summer traffic does not reach Blackdown, where the Hardy monument stands, and for those who wish to find a place where the whirr of an engine cannot be heard, the steep road from Blackdown to the Fleet and the sea may be the key to quietness. The Fleet is a long, narrow sheet of salt water which lies between the Chesil Bank and the mainland of Dorset. It stretches from the Swannery at Abbotsbury to the north end of Portland Isle. The shores of the Fleet opposite the Chesil Beach are low, and a line of detritus at low tide indicates a well-defined flow of sea-water into and out of the prisoned Fleet.

Many kinds of salt-loving plants flourish in the brackish mud of the landward edge of the Fleet, among them sea milkwort, bestarred in June and July with tiny, pinkish-helio flowers; altheæ, a beautiful rose-coloured mallow, whose stems and leaves, densely covered with fine silvery hairs, have a powdered or frosted look; green, glaucous suæda and fleshly triglochin over which none but botanists would dote. The sea-aster grows there as well—watercress, scurvy-grass, sea-rocket, wild celery, samphire and the maritime plantain. Among the bramble on the drier shore one may hear, and perhaps see, the ruddy-backed grass-hopper warbler singing its reeling song. Among the sea milkwort, triglochin and chocolate-tasselled scirpus of the beach an insect diet must be easy to find for the young birds. There is no sound save the lapping of the water, the call of the green plover, the reeling song of the warbler, or the grunt of a swan to the cygnets. No motor horn penetrates to this secluded spot.

On the beach the view seaward is bounded by the huge bank of pebbles. Beyond the bank is the open Channel. The waters of the Fleet, dotted about with queenly swans, shine like silver or gold in the summer sunlight. Even as one looks a creaking sound comes from over the Fleet. A swan has taken wing, another, and then another, and the queer rhythm of motion wheezes over the Fleet, and up the grassy slopes, as the sound beats back from the huge bank of pebbles. The creaking has a curious musical quality. The swan's flight has been described as making a whistling or crackling sound. As one listens on the beach the creaking acquires a liquid touch in its passage over the Fleet. Distance lends enchantment, for near at hand the swans' flight merely smacks of movement and has nothing vocal or metallic about it. When a pair of swans fly low over the surface of the sea, as they sometimes will in spring in an adventurous nuptial flight, and perchance are heard and seen from cliffs a hundred or so feet high, the creaking of the wings takes on a new and muffled tone unknown to the lesser heights by the Fleet.

Beyond the westernmost end of the Fleet, a broad bed of reeds, which covers acres of treacherous, brackish swamp, provides abundance of cover for coot and small reed-loving birds. Here, a pair of swans, wanderers from the Fleet, will occasionally make their home and rear young—not as outcasts but pioneers. What they lose by quitting their quarters at the Abbotsbury Swannery, is no doubt compensated by solitary life and rich, wild freedom—their motto 'odi profanum vulgus.'

The hamlet of East Fleet, now composed of a few small cottages has, in its day, met with high adventure. In times of terrific storm the sea now and again breaks over the Chesil Bank with great force, and the enormous volume of water thus thrown over into the Fleet, is prevented by the huge barrier of pebbles from going back with the receding wave. The imprisoned water sweeps over the low-lying land with catastrophic effect. In this way the village of East Fleet was invaded by the sea about a century ago, and its church and God's acre made desolate.

A path along the side of the Fleet follows the winding shore to West Fleet. In summer it runs by the edge of the golden corn which fills the loamy fields. Tall grasses cover the high bank which slopes sharply down from the path to the beach below. Mingling with the grasses and yellow spikes of toadflax are the delicate lilac flowers of slender flax plants. Though East Fleet with its deserted church be a spectacle of melancholy, West Fleet atones for the other by its green, umbrageous aspect. Beech or lime, fir and pine, vie with each other to make a shady retreat. The church, embowered in tall trees, stands solitary, lonesome, bereft. The greensward in early spring is ankle-deep in celandines, whose leaves and overgrown stalks in the month of May grow pallid in decay. The rich east window of the chancel is mainly green in colour, as if reflecting in its glass the umbrageous shade outside. Pinnacles on walls and tower are fashioned in pagoda style, and together with the battlements are softened by a veil of tender green thrown by the encompassing trees.

A winsome scene is that of the Fleet and the Chesil Bank which is presented to the onlooker on the top of Wear's Hill. The woods on the lower slope between the down and the pebble-bank, when, in spring, the pea-green tassels of the larch are flung against the dark green of the sombre pines, and both against the silver sea, are most wonderfully fair. Once in a while, perchance one may see a golden oriole fly hurriedly across the open slope towards the vari-coloured woods, his golden-yellow plumage vivid against the green of grass as he flies. The long, curved line of the opal-coloured Chesil Beach runs off to the left to Portland, the Fleet as an irregular watery streak in the rear, and on its front an arm of the boundless sea. The outlook is one of the fairest along the whole length of the south coast of England.

The witchery of the scene will be enhanced a hundredfold if one visits Wears Hill camp by the pale moonlight. Moonbeams glinting on the darkened sea and in the darker Fleet, take on a ghostly character when viewed from an elevation of several hundred feet. The fair, winsome scene of daylight resolves itself by night into a region of sinister aspect. Below, a steep road runs down to the murmuring sea beating dully upon the pebble beach. Above, where the rings of the ancient camp, ridge upon ridge, stand clear against the dimly star-lit sky, long-gone warriors come again and fight their age old battles. One may see them with the mind's eye—fierce, moving figures on the crests of the ridges, black against the sky, under the silent stars. The figures are speechless as the stars. There is none of the clash of battle, only the stark, dumb show, a witching mental product.

A keen perception of the need for defence on the seaward side had those men of other days, for the outlook from the camp sweeps the wide blue bay from Portland to Start Point. Not so much as a skiff would approach the Chesil Bank without being seen by the watchers on the down. What sort of people were they that the ancient tribes expected to attack their sun-kissed fortress? Would they float along the bay in coracles, in galleys, or in boats with bellying sails? The side of the fortress, which faces the river valley, is defended by ditch and ridge almost as deep and high as those on the seaward side.

From a corner of the roadway below Litton

Cheney the ridges of Wears Hill camp appear redoubtable even in the twentieth century. What enemies did the sturdy builders of the fortress fear from the green river valley ? Did Bride then flow serenely as it does to-day ? And the not far distant camp on Eggardon to the north—was it a friendly, an allied, or was it a rival camp ? It is impossible to answer such questions. One thing, however, is apparent. The race which built the camps was cradled in conflict amid dangers of an imminent kind.

A bank of pebbles would not on first thoughts seem likely to excite botanical interest of any sort. Yet the Chesil Beach yields a plant but rarely found on the coast of England. To see it in its natural haunt, a hard mile-long walk over shifty pebbles has to be undertaken. No tender-foot may find Pisum maritimum. The plant is commonly known as the sea-pea. Its other name of Lathyrus maritimus reveals relationship to the whole family of pea plants. The flowers are blue and are about the same size as the blossoms of the bush vetch. The leaves are a little larger than a farthing and nearly as round as that coin. They are thick and fleshy, and are salt-resisting like the leaves of most maritime plants. On the Chesil Beach the sea-pea grows between the silver waters of the Fleet and the sea. The pebbles here have swept upwards to a height of fifty feet above the brackish water on the one hand, and the salt water as of ocean on the other. Legend says that the sea-pea was established on the bank when famine stalked the land, and that it came as the gift of God like manna in the wilderness. It grows rarely on the coast of England, and is essentially a northern plant. The pods are from one or two inches long, each containing six or seven small peas. The outlook over the Channel at the point where the sea-pea grows is pleasant and refreshing. Landward the prospect is most wonderfully fair embracing terraced hills, one of which supports age-old St. Catherine's Church. The slopes of the fresh green, steeply-rising downs in spring are misty with the blue of hyacinths, and later pink-hazed by campions. From the top of the downs one may look upon the prostrate plants of sea-pea far below threading the pebble bank like a streak of green within a gem of moonstone.

CHAPTER IV

BEES AND BUTTERFLIES

THE highwater mark of luxury is, I think, to sit in warm sunshine on a green lawn in a garden chair, and watch the bees and butterflies that come within one's vision. The sky in summer and autumn has not, it is true, the superlative blue of spring, but the exquisite creatures which flit about the pink, flame, and wine-coloured snapdragons around the lawns of my garden are beautiful to behold. Snapdragons, did we say? Smart people and gardeners' catalogues call these plants antirrhinums. But a good Anglo-Saxon name often expresses the behaviour of a common English flower better than any other. Especially does this seem to be so when one watches the flowers busy at their snapping. Each pink dragon has two big lips, on the lower one of which a bee alights, and by pushing the upper lip opens the dragon's mouth. Then the bee crawls in and the two lips snap together behind it. Apparently it is all up with the little creature. When the honey has been stolen the insect begins to struggle for freedom. His legs first appear as the bee tries to come out backwards. Usually exit is made at the side of the dragon's mouth, as if the pink monster had lost some of its teeth there, though truth to tell, the bee merely follows the path of least resistance. The snap is strongest at the front of the dragon's mouth, where, as the bee enters, its back is flipped with the dragon's tongue and dusted with yellow pollen. While the bee thus occupies the shining hour, a faded, painted lady sips nectar from blue lobelias.

The butterfly has a broken wing from which three white spots have been torn away. Obviously she has lived! Does she realize her loss? She stays so long upon the flowers that one has opportunity to examine the wonderful coloured scales which make up her sum of beauty. A large insect, once a white butterfly, now a thing of 'shreds and patches,' alights also on the white-eyed blue flowers. A proud red admiral—almost as large and proud as others of his kind, which sun themselves upon the flaunting dahlias of the Dorchester public gardens—unfolds his richly-banded wings upon deep crimson asters, a very child of the sun. Small whites with black spots on the wings tussle in the air, just as they do by hundreds about the grassy rings of Maiden Castle—the famous camp two miles south of Dorchester. Next comes a flake of flying gold which gives the final touch, if, indeed, there can be finality in the realm of Nature, to a scheme of beauty beyond the art of man to contrive. It is a female clouded yellow butterfly, a thing of dreams rather than of reality. When the wings are closed, the hinder ones are seen to be of a delicate green colour underneath, with a ring or eye near the centre whose tints must have been gathered from the essence of ancient sunsets.

After the bees have worked their will with the pink, flame and wine-coloured snap-dragons, and the erstwhile busy, snapping lips have wilted and fallen to the ground, a new wonder is revealed. The pink dragons were, after all, only pawns in Nature's seasonal game of life. For the new wonder left visible by the dragon's fall, is to be found in monstrous pouches in the form of a fish's head. Each pouch has small, wide open apertures for mouth and eyes. Out of these when one holds the pouches the wrong way up comes tumbling a wealth of specie, for every pouch is full to overflowing. This wealth is not of silver and gold, but every minute token sent out in circulation from the pouches has the same superscription embossed upon it in fairly deep relief. They are small infinitesimal tokens, it is true, a nondescript brown in colour, and when exchanged for real coin cost a penny for two or three hundred. But through them, and the work of the bees, I can see banks and borders of my garden bright another summer with pink, flame, and wine-coloured dragons, beautiful, savage pawns blazoning their colours once more to further the production of specie. What a wonder there is, then, wrapped up in each little brown token, maintained in Nature's currency through cross-fertilization by a bee.

There are several kinds of bees which visit the snap-dragons in my garden. Among them, a small black velvet bee with yellow bands ; a large one twice as big as the first also with yellow bands —a sort of double-bee; a black bee with hinder part of abdomen grey; an all black velvet bee, small, but quick in flight, and bees of various sizes with brick-red abdominal bands. A few of these various kinds, notably those which have grey abdominal bands, bite the spur of the flower and extract honey secreted at the bottom of the tube without going into the dragon's mouth. The puncture made in the tube is visible to the unaided eye. These robber bees give nothing in return for the honey which they steal.

The painted lady butterfly is a rare visitor to the garden. In the rare years, when numbers of insects reach the coast, their beauty is seen to the best advantage on the sea-pinks which adorn the western end of the Chesil Beach. There they appear and vanish again with surprising rapidity, among the colours of the beach, as they alight with closed wings upon the pink flowers. The underside of the hind wings sometimes may have a pink patch upon it, which upon the sea-pinks explains the vanishing trick. The small copper butterfly, among the same coastal colours, alighting upon sea-pinks and tall maritime grasses is almost invisible with folded wings. On the helio Michaelmas daisies of my garden, this small butterfly with wings outspread is a conspicuous object. It will stay so long on one flower in the sun that one may count the spots on its wings. On every other flower a dipterous gem of the first water, with a body of shining emerald green, makes a fine foil for the copper of the butterfly. These green-bodied flies, sipping nectar from the yellow, tubular florets of the daisies, are vivid in the sunshine. There are, it may be, hundreds of them upon the numberless flowers.

Many butterflies are attracted by bright colours as well as by scent of flowers. Crimson escholtzias and bright-red candytuft, neither of them sweetly-scented species, when sown thickly upon a flower-bed, will attract other butterflies besides the usual inhabitants of a garden. Meadow browns, with orange patches, as well as a host of tortoise-shell butterflies, will play the livelong day about the showy blossoms, increasing the riot of colour.

The speckled wood butterfly, mentioned later in connexion with Lewesdon Hill, is a shade-loving species, which one may see, perchance, in the woods of Batcombe Down, and about the Great Ditch which skirts the southern side of that fine spur of chalk. Among furze, long grass and heather, fritillaries and skippers may be stalked, peacock butterflies, several at one time and together, I have seen on Lewesdon and on Thorncombe Beacon. One supposes that the metamorphosis from egg to butterfly must have taken place on the hills. The common nettle which is the host plant for the caterpillars, is found even on the highest hills. Among the bracken of Golden Cap, the highest point on the south coast, some six hundred feet above the sea, the peacock butterfly may be seen in summer. There, also, in the hot days of July a large, almost black butterfly, probably the variety nigrina of the white admiral, takes the air in rapid flight.

On steep slopes above the sea east of Burton Bradstock the largest fritillaries are to be met with in their proper season. Quantities of blues frequent the same locality together with meadow browns. On the pebble beach of Burton Freshwater among tall seaside grasses the small copper is regularly found. On the long stalks of grass the coppers, blues, small heaths and skippers are all alike invisible. Birdsfoot trefoil, the host plant of skipper and blue, abounds on the beach and the steep hillside. Docks there are also for caterpillars of the small copper.

Comma butterflies, which in 1926–7 frequented my garden, have since been remarkable for their absence. A few of these hibernated behind furniture in the house and came out in early spring, to be nipped with cold in the 'blackthorn winter.' The orange-tip butterfly, unlike the comma, seems to be increasing. Certain shady lanes from Whitechurch Canonicorum to Bothenhampton are their regular haunts. A dwarf butterfly of this type, with large orange tips considering its small size, was plentiful in 1930 in the sequestered village of Closworth. I saw the butterflies in a shady lane, full of rank growth, flitting about by the dozen. In the summer of the same year the brimstone butterfly was in evidence near Melbury Park, Lord Ilchester's beautiful home near Evershot, where a few delicate green females of this species were seen flying about the hedgerows. In a choice, little frequented lane, on the chalk lands leading down to a Roman road where spindle and buckthorn mingle together in the hedgerow, this beautiful creature may again be seen. A few butterflies of this species visit my garden in spring and summer. They do not stay as commas, and tortoiseshells and small coppers do. The black-veined white butterfly, and the marbled white, whose proper haunts are the higher chalk hills, occasionally stray down to my garden, probably from Eggardon Hill.

The wall butterfly, whether sunning itself in my garden or on mud banks down by the Fleet, is a quiet, unobstrusive creature which is easily overlooked. In gravel pits on Blackdown this butterfly looks its best. On Woodbury Hill, the scene of Greenhill Fair—where Gabriel Oak took Bathsheba's sheep for sale when managing her farm at Puddletown—I saw a gatekeeper butterfly which was but newly emerged from the chrysalis stage. The dark, sexual mark on the fore-wings common to this species, the meadow brown, and one or two other species, is one mark of recognition. The orange tints of this butterfly were bright, almost as the red of a small tortoiseshell when fresh and new. It was a remarkably beautiful example of the species to which it belonged.

CHAPTER V

THE BURIED PAST

WITHIN a day's journey of Port Bredy, where Lucetta of Casterbridge fame was married to Donald Farfrae, there are some twenty prehistoric camps on just as many hills. Each one of these has a story to tell, and each one is worth a separate journey and may be visited several times with pleasure. On seven only of these hills, or perhaps eight, does the roadway run within easy distance of the top. The remainder must be traversed laboriously on foot, from the roadway below, to the view point on vallum or tumulus. There is no royal road to the top. The traveller must labour for his pleasure. He will not grudge the exertion as ancient occupation reveals itself or the beauty of landscape unfolds. The writer has climbed toilsomely up each and every one of these hills, with a number of others, including Camelot outside the county boundary.

The two hills which present the stiffest tasks of all are Hod Hill and Hambledon, overlooking Blackmoor Vale. Of these two the view from Hambledon is to be preferred. It is very extensive, taking within its compass the western scarps of Cranbourne Chase. Melbury Hill, especially, looms grey and bare and lonesome to the east when seen from the ramparts of Hambledon Hill camp. The ramparts themselves are wonderful to behold. Running majestically along the whole length of the steep chalk slopes, now straight, now curved, according to the contour of the hill, one recalls no others like them—no, not even on the more distant Wiltshire Downs. If one climbs up to the ancient camp on Hambledon from the steep end at Child Okeford village, instead of approaching it from the natural entrance on the south-east, the grandeur of design of the earthen ramparts does indeed fill one with amazement. It excites admiration also for our ancestors of days long past. How they worked! How they strove! What did they do with those who would not give a helping hand? Those who wished to live without work? Short shrift, one thinks.

My memory of Hod Hill, Hambledon's near neighbour, is of a different sort. Let me say here that I made two journeys to Blackmoor Vale within a few days and devoted one day to each hill. Hurry is impossible on expeditions of this sort. My memory of Hod Hill is summed up chiefly in the botany of the hill top—in the beautiful spirea, S. filipendula, clustered bell-flowers, harebells, squinancy wort, the pale chalk scabious, S. columbaria, reddish-purple saw-wort, lemon hawk-weed and other gems of the plant world. The area of earth works being scheduled as a national monument, the whole is enclosed within a strong wire fencing and sheep are prevented from grazing on the turf. The result is a hill-top meadow of rare botanical quality.

Hambledon, on the other hand is grazed by cattle. From the scenic point of view Hod Hill loses something by the proximity of Hambledon. The shoulder of the latter hill hides the northern part of Blackmoor Vale and cuts the view off sharply against the savage-looking Melbury Hill. The earthworks of Hod Hill should, however, be seen by any one whose humour lies in the ancient history of our island.

The hill called Camelot, sometimes known as King Arthur's Castle, is in Somerset where that county touches the borders of Dorset. Other hills, green and rounded, stand hard by the hill of Arthurian legend. One of these is Corton Down on which the white meadow saxifrage, rare in southern counties, grows as it does also on Camelot. Lord Tennyson's king, the Arthur of legend, song, and story, is said to have been associated with Camelot Castle hill and with Badbury Rings in Dorset.

It was not until some eighty years ago that the camps of the down country aroused the curiosity of people capable of dealing with their secrets. Yet the veriest ignoramus would be brought to pause on ramparts like those of Camelot, and Hod and Hambledon hills. The deep, bare ditches of some of the many fortified hills, the confusion of rough growth, scrub and thicket which obscure the outlines of the defences of others, give ample food for thought. The ditches of the hill fort of Camelot or Cadbury Rings are still forty or fifty feet deep on the most strongly defended side. The hill is close to the village of South Cadbury, hence the name of Cadbury Rings sometimes given to the hill fortress. When I asked a native in the village, 'Do you call this hill Camelot?' the answer was in the affirmative. On the slope of the hill within the area of the fort King Arthur's well is pointed out by the villagers. Young cattle feed on the rough grass which grows between the tangle of ragwort, nettles and thistles within the camp on the top of the hill. They come down to drink at King Arthur's well. On the way down in wet weather, as they jostle each other through the levelled defences, they trample the white saxifrage, S. granulata, which grows here as on Corton Down, under their muddy hoofs. Legend, which says that Camelot was King Arthur's castle, holds that the great king met his death at Badbury Rings some twenty-five miles as the crow flies to the south-east of Camelot.

As sequestered Camelot is left behind one travels along secluded Somerset roads a mile or two to the Dorset boundary. A turn of the head on leaving the fortress reveals the rabbit-warrened ridges, and next the tree-crowned ramparts for many a mile. A little further and the hill takes on a kingly aspect. Again is it stately Camelot—the Camelot of chivalry, away there in the haze of a summer's day. Tennyson was right, for there are towers upon it now that were invisible when one was near. Distance lends enchantment and the mind can see what it will either past or present. Gone are the nettles and thistles and the rough young cattle that come down to drink at King Arthur's well. It is 'many-towered

Camelot' to which the patient Lady of Shallott looked, to her undoing, and its rings of trees hazy against a summer sky carry out the soft deception. The balmy, summer air, alive with hum of bee and click of out-door cricket, is full of bewitching romance. For the nonce, the greater antiquity of the ringed and crumbling fortress, is swallowed up in the poet's dream.

From Spettisbury Ring, another fortified hill above the Stour, a little more than half-way between Camelot and Badbury Rings, pine-crowned Mount Badon (so called) is seen in the distance on the other side of the river. The charming Stour is about two hundred feet below the bare, solitary ring of Spettisbury. In the days long gone, when hill camps were full of busy life, the ford across the shallows was commanded by the ring above the village of Spettisbury. Rush, sedge, and arrowhead grow eight, nine or ten feet high in the sluggish water near the bridge which spans the river at the ford. The bridge is a fine old structure of nine arches through which in winter pour the waters of Blackmoor Vale.

To the uninitiated the term 'Rings' used to describe many prehistoric camps of the down country may appear obscure. The Rings of these early fortresses are distinct from the Roman fosse and vallum. They are a series of earthen ridges, with ditches between, thirty, forty or fifty feet high and deep. These ramparts run round the top of the hill following the contour whether round, oval, or rectangular. Inside the outer ring and ditch there is another ring of equal height, or higher than the outer ring, and then another ditch. Inside these a third ring and ditch protect the inner camp. At the entrance to the camps there are usually other intricate defences. Badbury Rings are of the same type as the fortress of Camelot.

Pine-crowned Badbury, whose origin is lost in antiquity, though easy of approach, has a remoteness peculiar to itself. It is on the edge of Cranborne Chase. At a time of approaching storm the loneliness of the great earthwork is something which can be felt. When thunder clouds come down and sweep over the rings, touching them as they go, or drag their ragged edges along the tops of the trees in the avenue on the Wimborne-Blandford road at the bottom of the greensward, one realizes the elevation of the rings, it may be, for the first time. A thunder-storm on Yarnbury Castle on the high, bare chalk downs, where forked flashes appear to touch the ground in quick succession, is more rousing because more intimate and menacing. On Badbury Rings the trees must bear the brunt of the storm while the onlooker watches the play. On the bare chalk downs the traveller feels himself a partici-pator in the tempest. On Badbury Rings when the sun shines brightly, and pink-veined squinancy dots the close-cropped greensward, the lemon hawkweed, rich and cheerful, spreads out its strap-shaped petals, then the scene is pleasant indeed. The cluster of pine-trees on the top of Badbury Rings is the haunt of woodland birds. The author of *The Green Roads* mentions this wood as the last nesting place of wild ravens in England. I doubt the correctness of that conclusion.

Only a few years ago I saw ravens in the breeding season about the screes of Wastwater. There is a tradition mentioned also in the book referred to, that one day 'Arthur shall come again.' Until that time the great king's soul must live in the body of a raven. The tradition apparently held that the soul of Arthur took wing and flew away with the ravens when he was mortally wounded on Badbury, or on Badon Hill. The legend appears to infer that pine-trees grew on Badbury Hill at a very remote period. In the deep ditches between the Rings where the invader vanquished the fortress-builders, pink and white wild roses bloom oblivious of ancient human drama. The ridges support the red-tasselled salad burnet in summer and orchises in the spring. The formal candelabra of pale blue or silver gentians hold minute corpse-candles in autumn as they have done for many and many a year on the Rings—not one only, but an incalculable number for every warrior who fell done to death in the ditches.

The two highest hills of Dorset are Lewesdon and Pilsdon Pen. Both rise abruptly above the beautiful vale of Marshwood, and are scarcely more than two miles apart. Pilsdon Pen is bare save for its encirclement of ancient defences. Lewesdon is mantled with trees. From Pilsdon a wide expanse of the Channel may be seen on the south and the distant Mendips touching the sky on the north. Level-topped Racedown above the house of that name is the westernmost point of the Pilsdon Range. Wide green trackways through the bracken on Racedown seem to indicate the course taken by racehorses of other, bygone days. No races are held on the broad hilltop to-day.

Lewesdon is the second highest hill in Dorset. Traces of an ancient camp in banks and ditches are to be found near the top of the hill, the banks overgrown with scrub and brambles. The sloping slides of the steep hill are covered with tall beech trees, and last year's layer of fallen leaves lies brown upon the floor of the wood. The soil of the ancient trackways under the old trees is fine and dry as flour and the feet sink softly in. So dense is the wood, where glades covered with bracken or bramble are hemmed round by a ring of trees, that the company of an uninvited sheep dog may be very welcome. Here is an intelligent fellow of old Dorset breed who shows much uneasiness if my companion and I when climbing the hill get a little apart from each other. In the ancient banks are holes of badger, fox, and weasel and probably of the herbivorous rabbit, too. What weird screams must be heard in the night when wild creatures prey upon each other. One keeps to the trackway in order to avoid holes which are hidden by a dense carpet of twigs and leaves covering the wood floor to a depth of several inches. Great fan-shaped clumps of ferns of wonderful grace and beauty grow on the higher slopes of the hill—buckler ferns, shield ferns, male ferns, and lady ferns of a delicate tender green. Through the beech trees bands of brilliant sunshine fall across the ferns on the slopes. The summit is a narrow, grass and bramble-covered plateau about a hundred and fifty yards long. Over the tops of pine and beech there is a beautiful prospect of green hills and valleys where Dorset meets Devon.

In the distance are the sea-cliffs about Lyme Regis, where Jane Austen got inspiration for *Persuasion*, the last of her various novels. But the kindly sheep-dog, who has accompanied us up the hill, disturbs the soothing noonday silence by barking savagely at the low-growing, lordly beeches below, on the steepest side of the hill. Their lowest branches almost sweep the ground. As I look down among and under them as well as the deep shade will allow, I see nothing but rich girth of trunks and a carpet of dark brown leaves. Does the intelligent animal, with a vision keener than my own, see shades of Neolithic man who, with great labour built ancient fortresses of earth? At any rate, to that one point under the beeches he looks from time to time and barks each time he looks, as if something ghostly were visible there. The sun shines brightly on the plateau on the top of the hill, and human thought apprehends nothing, but the sheep-dog whose name even I do not know refuses to be consoled.

On the south side of the hill where a belt of stunted trees grows about the crumbled defences there is ‘a bank where the wild thyme blows’—a bank which might have been the one that Oberon knew. The air is full of the fragrant

SPETTISBURY BRIDGE, NORTH SIDE

scent, and the slender trailing branches mix freely with the prostrate speedwell which partly covers the bank with tiny pale green purses. In a shady lane below, the speckled wood butterfly may be taken by hand, so leisurely is its flight. In autumn acorns are large and green on the low oaks of the hedgerows, and the scarlet berries of honeysuckle peep out from the tops of trees—holly, beech, or blackthorn.

In West Dorset there are two other fortified hills that, like Pilsdon Pen and Lewesdon, overlook the beautiful Marshwood Vale—the home of yellow daffodils which 'take the winds of March with beauty.' The two fortified hills are Lambert's Castle hill and Coney's Castle, the term castle in each case referring to the prehistoric entrenchments still fairly well preserved. On the racecourse on Lambert's Castle horse-racing is an annual fixture. The prospect from the hill at various points is remarkably fine, and on the seaward side is said to be the finest in the county.

Coney's Castle hill is a lesser height. The defences on the seaward side are very steep and must in their day have been unassailable. It is the most picturesque of the four fortified hills of West Dorset. It is not a racecourse like Lambert's Castle hill, nor treeless like Pilsdon Pen. Its tangle of growth is rarely impenetrable, like the bramble, holly and blackthorn scrub which clings to the slopes of Lewesdon. Coney's Castle is a poet's hill whose 'crowded hour of glorious life' passed with King Egbert's defeat by the so-called savage Dane. Its epic is unwritten. It is less known than the higher, more notable hills. It is more secluded. The roads which approach it are models of rusticity. One may walk along ancient defences facing a sun-lit sea, under straggling chestnuts for whose presence here Romans were probably responsible. One has to remember that these ancient fortresses were used by every tribe that held power in the country, from the hillmen, down to the Saxon of historic times. On the soft leaf-mould of the defences in the wood great clusters of the fern Lastrea dilatata, with fronds three or four feet long, uplift one with a sense of the beauty of form. The tops of the earthen banks are strewn in autumn with the prickly fruit of sweet chestnuts. If one follows the bank, to the edge of the wood on the top of a precipitous slope, to draw apart the boughs of trees as one would draw back a curtain, a village on Lyme Bay bursts upon the vision. Between the bay and Coney's Castle every possible shade of brown, green, russet and corn colour is marshalled for inspection in the landscape. Overhead in the trees the crackling and snapping of wings indicates that ring-doves have been disturbed by human voices below. A few of their pale and dark grey feathers lie on the banks among prickly fruit of sweet chestnuts. Like the beech trees on Lambert's Castle and on Lewesdon Hill, the trees on Coney's Castle are the haunt of ring-doves, whose lovesome cooing is as characteristic as the startling snap of the wings.

The great camp on Eggardun Hill, near Powerstock, must, in the days of the hillmen, have been one of the most important in the county. The southern ramparts are even now clearly defined to the traveller on the highway over the Dorset heights. The hill—a great spur of chalk, much elevated above the surrounding country—is the westerly limit of the chalk formation in the county. Its use as a fortress at a much later date in history than the days of the hillmen, is probably indicated in its name, a softened form of the less euphonious Edgar's Down. Edgar was King of Mercia before he became King of Wessex, and why his name should be given to this hill is not clear. There is no record of a battle fought upon its steeply sloping sides in Saxon times.

But, about the same period, Idwal, a chief among Welshmen, whose sons became kings, gave his name to one of Cambria's most sombre lakes, the dream-like Llyn Idwal in its darkly rocky setting. The memory of Gunnar, one of the greatest of the Norsemen, is perpetuated in Gunnerside, a Yorkshire hill, with which for desolation Eggardun can in no way compare. Kingly names for outstanding natural features were evidently fashionable at the period.

Sea- and land-scapes in summer, as seen from Eggardun's bold brow are remarkably fine. On three sides of the great camp the ground slopes sheer down to the valleys below where no rivers wind their way. There is a small stream on the northern side and another which proceeds from chalk-bound Askerswell along the southern side of the hill. Dragon flies, both blue and golden brown, haunt the boggy ground at the foot of the hill.

In rare plants characteristic of a chalk or limestone formation Eggardun is not rich. A low growing form of marjoram is to be found upon the hill, and the field gentian grows on the north or eastern slope. Species of the less rare orchises are sought, such as the pyramid, the fragrant orchis and ophrys apifera.

Perhaps the finest view of Eggardun is to be got from Powerstock churchyard, where a yew tree on the one hand and the old church on the other frame the distant hill between them. But the great camp of the hillmen goes unbeknown and unsuspected from the elevated greensward where sleep the dead from the village below.

Chapter VI

RACEDOWN

A LOVER of poetry would naturally turn over once again the pages of Wordsworth's poems before visiting Racedown—a spot hallowed by the memory of that master of our English tongue. Newer poets have arisen ere now, it is true, but the Lakeland star shines brightly as ever, the clear white light eclipsed by no other. One glorious day of a St. Luke's summer the October sunlight streamed through the beeches on the lawn at Racedown in shafts of orange and of yellow light. Phrases from the poems come readily to mind as one sees the lofty trees, the bold front of the house, the garden about which Dorothy Wordsworth once walked arm in arm with the poet. The Tintern Abbey poem reveals what his sister's friendship was to William Wordsworth at Racedown as well as in Somerset.

> For thou art with me, here upon the banks
> Of this fair river, thou my dearest friend,
> My dear, dear friend, and in thy voice I catch
> The language of my former heart, and read
> My former pleasures in the shooting lights
> Of thy wild eyes. Oh ! yet a little while
> May I behold in thee, what I was once,

> My dear, dear sister ! and this prayer I make
> Knowing that nature never did betray
> The heart that loved her ; 'tis her privilege
> Through all the years of this our life, to lead
> From joy to joy.

Where shall one find a love-lilt half so sweet as this ? In Shakespeare's sonnets ? Ah, no ! They are redolent with a motive that does not enter here. To Beatrice ? Ah, no, again ! Dorothy is human. Her eyes have shooting lights. She is not idealized, beatified, as was the shade of Dante's heroine walking in paradise. There is Hope, to be sure, sweet, bright-eyed Hope, with the 'silver pinions,' on whom Keats calls in supplication with the most fascinating affection. But she is a goddess—the sheen of whose pinions 'fills the skies with silver glitterings.' Yet, stay, are not those silver glitterings of the same essence as the shooting lights from Dorothy Wordsworth's eyes ? Of the same essence as sunshine glinting on the green polished leaves of trees, and shrubs, and plants ; of the colours of the rainbow of moon-light on the sea ? Of the golden and orange sun-light streaming through the beeches ?

While these thoughts were passing through my mind there came a change over the face of Race-down. No longer did the poet walk arm in arm with Dorothy under the beeches and round about the garden paths. The *Lyrical Ballads* them-selves, inspired by the scenery and atmosphere of the glorious western slope of Pilsdon Pen, the Tintern one with the rest, were suddenly forgotten.

Racedown was no longer musical Racedown, of pure Saxon origin. It had become the pretentious Kellynch Hall, and inside was Sir Walter Eliot brimful of vanity, turning over the leaves of *The Baronetage* as he had been for quite a century past. There, too, was the stately Elizabeth, his eldest daughter, handsome like himself, at a dangerous age for a spinster with no suitor on the horizon. There she was in pink frock, walking in the garden on the morning after the dance. Along the drive came the cousin, who would succeed to the estate, and whom Elizabeth meant to marry whether he wished it or not. At least so I dreamed until light foot-falls roused me from abstraction and quickly I turned half expecting to see Anne Eliot, Jane Austen's own self coming round the bend in the roadway. But it was only the brown and yellow leaves of autumn that, elfinlike, had tripped along behind, tapping lightly on the ground as they came. And when I looked back to the lawn, the orange sunlight of an October sun was streaming through the beeches still.

It was in the West Country that Wordsworth learned to think that 'every flower enjoys the air it breathes,' for the 'Lines written in early spring' were prompted by some nook near Racedown, or the poet's later home in Somerset. Holford Glen, near Alfoxden, has been named by a writer on the Quantocks as the 'bower' where 'the periwinkle trails its wreaths.' The author did not state whether or no the periwinkle still grew there. To gratify my curiosity on the matter, a journey was made to the Somerset glen a few years ago. It was found that the long stems and glossy leaves of the plant did indeed trail over the steep banks of the glen as they may have done for a century past. Beneath the brambles they wind about with a persistence that promises well for another hundred years. The sides of the glen consist of the characteristic red earth of Somerset.

Holford is so near to Alfoxden, that the distance would be trifling to a poet who strode the Quantock country to Nether Stowey and back again several times a week. As a wilding the lesser periwinkle occurs also in Dorset. Therefore is it possible that in some Dorset nook thoughts and feelings were engendered which found expression in the 'Lines written in early spring,' though the poem might be written in Somerset. Goody Blake, one of the *Lyrical Ballads* written at Alfoxden, was unquestionably reminiscent of the poet's life at Racedown. Dorset was mentioned in an early draft of the poem. 'The Borderers' on the other hand, though written at Racedown, where soft western breezes blow, has the sharpness of the keen cutting winds of the Cheviot Hills, whose wild scenery is depicted throughout the play. An argument of time and place is of no avail, it may be said, in seeking for the fountain of a poet's inspiration. Yet it is fraught with absorbing interest to the earnest student of the Cumberland poet's works. The trailing periwinkle is, apparently, the only token by which Holford Glen has been singled out as the place of origin of the 'Lines written in early spring.' Far away in Cumberland I saw the lesser periwinkle growing as late as 1914 at a spot where in Wordsworth's youthful days the remnants of an avenue or grove probably stood. The poet's plant grew in 'a grove' wherein he 'sat reclined.' Holford Glen will scarcely bear such a pleasing description.

On the banks of a tributary of the river Eden, which rises in the Crossfell range of the Pennine Chain, at one time a nunnery stood. Croglin Water, for that is the name of the tributary stream, emerges from a deep gorge as a rushing mountain torrent, leaping from heights to lower heights until it assumes a pastoral aspect, singing as it goes over stones and pebbles. Shortly afterwards its highest point of grandeur is reached. From fields where it flows limpidly on lapping alders and willows, it plunges into a canyon some eighty feet deep, and after a series of rapids and strids resumes its pastoral aspect. The canyon is half-a-mile long. Upon the banks of Croglin Water the nunnery walks extend the whole length of the ravine, carved out of the solid rocks and overhung by them and by trees.

The ravine would scarcely measure thirty feet across. The roar of the falling waters fills the canyon at its commencement where it is most enclosed, and the ground beneath one's feet vibrates as the water pours into a huge rock basin. The nuns' walks are guarded by iron railings in dangerous places. In stormy weather, when Croglin is in spate, the rock path must be impassable. At the end of the ravine the wood thins out, and the ground is overgrown with cowslips, hyacinths or bluebells and other woodland gems.

There, too, in the woods 'the periwinkle trails its wreaths.' The poet knew Croglin Water. He wrote a sonnet with the nunnery for its theme. Who, then, shall say that some memory of this spot did not prompt the 'Lines written in early spring,' though written in the West Country? Through the red earth of Holford Glen and the trailing periwinkle, the poet may have seen that other red earth of his beloved river Eden, where also 'the periwinkle trails its wreaths,' and in the poem the transmutation is as beautiful as it is complete. The sonnet on the nunnery, it is true, was written at a later date, as well as the one on the Eden, but the latter river had been the poet's 'life's neighbour' to whom, belated, he pays 'dues of neighbourhood.' What further proof need we that the poet knew Croglin Water in his youth?

At Lyme Regis, by the sea, some half dozen miles from Racedown, there is an old bow-window in a house on the beach, through which Jane Austen must have watched the breakers of Lyme Bay beat savagely on the shore. It was there that *Persuasion* was conceived if not written —the last, and perhaps the sweetest of her several novels.

CHAPTER VII

INTERESTING CHURCHES

It would be a thankless task to have to say which was the most interesting church in Dorset, for just as York Minster is the noblest cathedral in England, though most others of our cathedrals have some point of superiority over the great Northern Minster, so most Dorset churches have some distinction not possessed by any of the rest. One possession is common to many of the churches of the land of the ancient Durotriges, and that is a Norman font. It may be that no other county is so rich in such small remains of our historic Norman past. The iconoclastic restorer of church architecture, deservedly ostracized in one of Thomas Hardy's poems, seems to have held his hand in Dorset. The churches of the county are worthy of a round trip for the study of fonts alone. Compared with the famous, richly-carved fonts of the country, such as the one in East Dereham Church, the Norman basins of Dorset are plain and restrained in the extreme.

In the little edifice of Winterbourne Monkton, which lies deep below the southern ramparts of Maiden Castle, there is a semi-recumbent figure of one, Ella, sculptured in a flesh-coloured marble. The figure reclines in an alcove of the chancel. The sculpturing of the hands and fingers—the second hand is behind the head—is such as to arrest attention. The posture, for a memorial figure recumbent, is an unusual one. The church of Winterbourne Came—a village which derives its name from the same 'winter burn' as the last—is notable for having had as incumbent for many years the Rev. William Barnes, the much-loved Dorset poet. He was a Dorset man who sang sweetly of Blackmoor Vale in poems of choice words and flowing measure. A monumental stone to his memory, bound all about with a cable design cut into and out of the stone, stands in the lone, damp ground close by the old church tower. The memorial has a form approaching a Latin cross, and the carving at a distance suggests a Runic design of figures. The extensive and intricate use of the cable style of decorative carving gives this first impression. It is intended to convey the same meaning as the use of the vine in carving—'the true vine,' a purely spiritual conception. A hempen cable lends itself to much artistic knotting and coiling. It is beautifully employed in a number of places in Dorset. A singularly fine example is to be found on a very old headstone at the remote village of Rampisham, an old Roman station away in the hills where infant Froom flows down its narrow bed.

The interest of Winterbourne Steepleton, a village on the same 'burn' as the two already mentioned, lies in the mediæval stone spire of its church, an old Norman font, and a little ancient glass in the small upper lights of one or two of the northern windows. This old glass is palish-yellow in colour and apparently represents the newly-risen sun. Old glass of the same kind and design, and doubtless of the same age, is to be seen in a window of Marnhull Church in Blackmoor Vale, the Marlott of *Tess of the d'Urbervilles*. In its utter simplicity this glass is more in keeping with the Spartan plainness of the Steepleton Church than with the elaborate edifice of Marnhull. A note, which lies upon the ancient font, that he who runs may read, is a timely help for a proper appreciation of the little old church by the willows. How softly the centuries must have passed over its head! The eyes of thousands of tourists rest upon it for an instant in the long days of spring and summer as they pass, in sunshine and in shower. Little they know that the adjacent willows encompass so ancient a shrine.

At Coombe Keynes, near Lulworth, where the church was rebuilt in the last century, there is some old painted glass. The east window in style and colouring is suggestive of the old glass at Steepleton, but the figures on the Coombe Keynes' window are of a more ornamental type, and are repeated in each of the several lights. Winterborne Abbas and Martinstown, two other villages upon the same 'winter burn' as Steepleton, each possesses a Norman bowl big enough for the reception of infants at baptism. It is a notable fact that most of these old fonts are sufficiently deep and wide to allow of complete immersion. Probably immersion was the recognized method of baptism at that period of church history when these Norman fonts were cut, often from one block of local or of Purbeck stone.

It is not necessary to enumerate all the Norman fonts in the county, but they are to be found in places unlike as Affpuddle, hidden in Egdon Heath, and Studland on the regular tourist track. There is a font of Norman type at Bere Regis, and a Norman bowl at Puddletown, the Kingsbere and Weatherbury respectively of the Hardy novels. The interest of the Bere Regis Church lies in its association with the great Turberville family, once very powerful in Dorset, and with that widely read romance *Tess of the d'Urbervilles*. The lion rampant of the richly-coloured Turberville windows of Bere Regis Church has its counterpart on an inn signboard some little way from Wool Bridge, or Wellbridge, a sure proof of deep roots in the history of the district. The lion is a proud figure even when detached from the rich colouring of ecclesiastical windows. There is nothing hackneyed about the Turberville beast of prey. His attitude suggests a bold, ramping creature full of hot blood and combative energy, surely a trustworthy emblem of the ancient Turberville spirit. The roof of Bere Regis Church is a survival of barbaric splendour. Its ornamentation is totally un-English. By comparison with the chaste fan-vaulted roof of Sherborne Abbey, or the ancient one of the Somerton fane, richly carved by Muchelney monks, the roof of Bere Regis Church appears fantastical. One learns with no surprise that it was imported from the Continent by a Roman Catholic priest. Simple richness of blue ceiling, such as that of Huish Episcopi just over the Somerset border, does not here shed sweetness and light. The Bere Regis ceiling is, however, frequently described as handsome. As a historical monument the church may be impressive or expressive according to the onlooker's turn of thought.

The vision of Fanny Robin conjured up by memory on a visit to the old church of Puddletown, the Weatherbury of Bathsheba and Gabriel Oak, is not a pleasing one. The gargoyle, which poured water into the grave of the erring girl, is not on Puddletown Church. Gargoyles there are in plenty in Dorset capable of the devastating operation described by the novelist, in places remote from the busy highway. Within the church there is a Norman font decorated with symbolic carving of the vine which, like the coiled cable design, is intended to convey an idea of the divine love twining over and about all life.

The memorial window to Thomas Hardy, novelist and poet, in the southern wall of the church at Stinsford, the Mellstock of the novels, is beautiful in execution. The figure in the central light, resplendent in purple mantle, seems to suggest that the great novelist was in the direct succession of the great line of prophets. Yet through the ether, ere the novelist's heart was cold, a man hesitated not to broadcast his opinion that Thomas Hardy would be forgotten within a quarter of a century. One wonders what that individual would offer to have the speech 'unsaid'! Deep in the God's acre of Stinsford Church that wonderful heart lies buried, resting for ever, one likes to think, upon the breast of Elfrida, the blue-eyed lodestar of his youth.

Several village churches, especially near Port Bredy, are fortunate in the possession of an avenue of yew-trees leading to the door of the church. At St. Mary's, Port Bredy, a yew avenue of some age runs from the porch to the vicarage. Burton Bradstock, a village near the little port, possesses such a dark-hued avenue, along which even a bride must walk. Symondsbury, likewise, has a yew avenue, from the door to a side gateway. Marnhull, in Blackmoor Vale has an avenue of yews along a quiet sidewalk. These trees are none of them of sufficient antiquity to be associated with bow and arrow days, but the fine old yew tree of Stoke Abbot, and the spreading yew tree of Broadwindsor, both have their origins in a far distant past. A yew tree with a circumference of twenty-eight feet was blown down at Sturminster Marshall in the Stour valley in 1832—a hundred years ago. It is not clear whether or no this enormous tree grew in the churchyard of the village, but in 1860 the church was rebuilt. The bare contemplation of this giant among yews brings to mind Wordsworth's dramatic picture of noon-tide under the yew-trees where ghostly shapes may meet :

> Fear and trembling Hope
> Silence and Foresight—Death the Skeleton
> And Time the Shadow,—there to celebrate
> United worship ; or in mute repose
> To lie, and listen to the mountain flood
> Murmuring from Glaramara's inmost caves.

PORTESHAM CHURCH

Many village churches of Dorset in the Perpendicular style are of considerable interest on account of their imposing towers—imposing, that is to say in the unusual setting of a quiet rural landscape. One of these at Beaminster, the imaginary home of Angel Claire, has a tower in the Tudor style overloaded with ornament. From the high down—Toller or Beaminster Down—the lofty tower set in the midst of trees makes a charming picture of rural peacefulness, such as one might expect to see when emerging from a roadway lined by tiers of foxgloves, rich in purple fingers. Other Perpendicular churches, such as Charminster, Whitechurch, Bradford and Cerne are of a more reserved type. Each one is worthy of a whole leisure hour and more—Bradford Abbas and Charminster for beauty of architecture and dignity of Gothic style, Cerne Abbas and Whitechurch for history and charm of situation. Bradford Abbas is in the north of the county on the Somerset border, and possesses a singularly pleasing exterior as it stands in solitary dignity in the midst of a matter-of-fact village. Both of these churches, as well as many another village church of Dorset and of Somerset, were obviously built for a far greater population than can be found surrounding them to-day. Some sort of industry, which has long ceased to exist, must have bound together communities which required edifices so stately as those of Cerne, Charminster and Huish, to quote no others. It has to be remembered, however, that in ancient days attendance at church was compulsory, just as attendance at school is compulsory for children to-day. The education of the rank and file was derived from the teaching of the pulpit. Over all knowledge, therefore, was cast an ecclesiastical colouring, emanating in the first place from abbey, priory and nunnery. Compulsory attendance at church necessitated buildings big enough to hold the people of the parish, and the kindly hand of Father Time has bequeathed much of the fabric to later generations.

The church of Whitechurch Canonicorum in Marshwood Vale, the haunt of daffy-down-dilly, possesses a Norman nave. One of the columns supporting the roof on the southern side leans outwards at an angle of several degrees. Two of the round arches which carry the curve from one Norman column to another are thus thrown out of shape. In spite of these facts the structure is perfectly rigid, the leaning column being stabilised by strong stonework. There is an old shrine in the northern transept said to be the tomb of St. Candida, a half-forgotten saint. More interesting still is a stone in the outer wall of the church on which the carving of a chalice or 'holy grail' is visible. No legend seems to attach to this remarkable figure. The carving is rather crude in outline and is apparently about the same age as the gargoyles which adorn the church, though the motive for the carving of the grail must have been different from that which led to the inception of a gargoyle. Reverence would prompt the first, and a pawky humour the second, unless,

RESTORED CROSS, CORFE MULLEN

indeed, the gargoyle was meant to intimidate the feeble-minded.

The church of Broadwindsor under Lewesdon Hill on the north, and the smaller one of Stoke Abbott under Lewesdon on the south-east, each has a Norman font. Each also once had for rector a noted man of letters—Thomas Fuller and the poet Crowe respectively. These two churches together with Whitechurch and Thorncombe—form a group in West Dorset interesting in detail and picturesque in situation. There is a Norman aisle and an Early English aisle at Broadwindsor, and a Jacobean pulpit from which Thomas Fuller preached. A strong box in the vestry contains this author's works. Thorncombe, said to be one of the prettiest of Dorset villages, has two fourteenth-century brasses in its church, memorials to Sir Thomas and Lady Brook. The latter, in a winged head-dress makes an engaging figure.

The beautiful figure of Lady Brook in brass in Thorncombe Church carries the mind to Abbotsbury, where a painted St. Catherine in a stained glass window on the south side of St. Michael's Church exceeds in beauty of outline the memorial brass of Lady Brook. The hands of the saint on the glass, folded together as in prayer, are exquisite in form. This representation of St. Catherine was taken from the ruin of the church of her name on the hill above the Fleet. The walls of this old ruin, which has survived many centuries are several feet thick, reinforced by strong buttresses on the outside. The necessity for this great strength was made manifest in the heavy gales of 1929, when the walls of a church near the coast, in a similar exposed position and which were not so strengthened, cracked before the onslaught of fierce winds. Both Abbotsbury Church and the ruined St. Catherine's belong to the Perpendicular style, the latter having probably been a beacon tower, or a chapel of thanksgiving like the strange little ruin of St. Gabriel under Golden Cap. The church of St. Michael at Abbotsbury has recently been restored, and during restoration two Commonwealth bullets were found in the roof. Two holes in the Jacobean pulpit are said to date from the same stormy period.

Portisham, the native village of Captain Hardy of Trafalgar fame, whose letter to his country on the death of Nelson is in the museum at Dorchester, boasts some Early English windows in its church. With its old porch and ivy-mantled tower the church makes an attractive picture in the midst of an old-time village. Rampisham Church also is mainly Early English in style, though wear and tear of chiselled stonework is not apparent here as it is at Portisham, where the Gothic window tracery appears to be crumbling to decay. The salt sea air which may reach Portisham from the south-west, in time eats into the hardest stone, bringing about disintegration. Rampisham beyond the great bulk of Toller Down is past the touch of sea air.

Among the churches of Dorset which have Early English features of some importance Corfe Mullen must be remembered for its general quaintness.

It is a church that ought to be seen by all lovers of ancient things and ancient usages. It is easy to imagine the poor children of other days going out from the old church at the close of morning service, to the stone at the village cross, where an allowance of bread and cheese was distributed every week.

The apsidal chancel of the beautiful church of Cattistock, reminiscent in a small way of the magnificent one of Lichfield Cathedral, does much credit to rectors past and gone, whose duty it used to be to keep the chancel in repair in all English churches. The graceful tower of this church, rising clear among the hills as one descends upon the village from Rampisham, is very pleasing, especially so when the music of the chiming bells is carried through the upland valley. The delicately-toned carillon of thirty-five bells was cast in Louvain.

Two other churches within the county which have Early English features must not be forgotten—the secluded one of Up Cerne, in its sylvan retreat amid bare chalk hills, and Powerstock Church, on its little hill at the head of the shady valley down which flows the Mangerton stream. Though small the well-kept church of Up Cerne possesses an ancient dignity. The windows are all of interest. One, a memorial window bearing figures 1914-18, displays St. George slaying a red-skinned and red-mouthed dragon, a creature 'red in tooth and claw.' In a combe of the Quantock Hills the same subject, upon a memorial tablet of the same period, is represented in bright metal colourings on marble, but in the latter case the redness of tooth and claw is not apparent. The monster's worst appearance of savagery is delicately concealed by closed jaws. The mouth of the Up Cerne dragon is wide open. The treatment of the subject here does not convince one of the dragon's utter defeat. The latter, one fears, is both futurist and prophetic. Another of the Up Cerne windows bears a painting of the Christ amidst lilies of the field, a full-length figure clear and distinct from its surroundings. Portraits of this kind, if they may be so called, are very effective. The Briton, Roman and Saxon of a window in Wareham Church epitomizes not only the past history of Dorset but of the whole of England. The figures of Joseph of Arimathea, St. Christopher, St. Catherine and Francis of Assisi in the church of Minehead make up a fine study in this type of window. So, too, do the many fine groups in the old church of Bishop's Lydeard—Sarah and Isaac, Eunice and Timothy, Moses, Elijah, together with King Alfred of Wessex. Simeon and Elizabeth of Stogumber Church, two rare figures upon glass, must also be remembered here.

We have already mentioned that the church of Powerstock stands upon a hill—or, to be scrupulously correct—on an eminence among the hills which rises abruptly in the midst of the village. It is a very good and a very interesting specimen with some Early English features and many richly-coloured windows. It possesses a marble font, new, but chaste, modelled on the old cracked

Norman bowl which stands hard by it within the shelter of the church. There is something particularly pleasing in this evidence of good taste in copying the old anew.

The *piece de resistance* of Powerstock Church is the chancel arch of Norman workmanship of the eleventh century. It is a semi-circular threefold arch. Three types of decorative carving appear on the three arches, and on the columns which support them the designs characteristic of Norman columns are to be seen. The inner arch is carved in a bold pattern resembling an enveloping cable, but no strands or fibres of a cable are visible in the carving. This was a device used both in the Norman and Lombardic styles of the Romanesque in architecture, for doorway or arch. In it one may see, perchance, the origin of the decorative carving on tombstones alluded to at the beginning of this chapter. What its symbolism stands for, here in the chancel arch, is not easy to understand. Perhaps the intent was purely decorative, for figures of lengths of cable and of links of chain were common in Roman mosaic pavements, as were many other patterns found upon Norman ecclesiastical columns.

The second or middle semicircle of the threefold arch is decorated with figures which approximate to the spreading petals of a flower such as stitchwort or ranunculus. The origin of this type would probably be found in the figure of the wheel of fortune, which was often used to deck Roman altar or memorial. Very old gravestones in many places in Dorset have a similar figure on them.

The outer or uppermost semicircle of the arch is made up of a series of zig-zag lines running the whole curved length of the arch. These lines in the hands of the ancient Greeks, who never made an arch, had appeared in designs of great beauty for columns, the zig-zag lines having between them a thin-lined scroll pattern. The pattern of the scroll appears, if I remember rightly, on one of the columns which support the chancel arch. Of how venerable a lineage are those simple Norman designs!

CHAPTER VIII

CROSSES AND GARGOYLES

THE old stone crosses of Dorset may not be said to rival those of Somerset or of some other counties. There was originally a widely distributed type which might be described as ecclesiastical in aspect, but all have disappeared save the fourteenth-century cross which stands in the main street of Stalbridge. A niche on these crosses was usually filled by a figure of the crucified Christ. A modern example of this type of cross has been erected at Gillingham in the extreme north of the county, as a war memorial. The fitness and good taste of this tribute to the dead are qualities which have been but rarely exercised in the erection of memorials to the lost in the Great War. The restraint of the Gillingham memorial, modelled so chastely on the old type of cross, comes as balm to the wounded spirit.

In the *Antiquities of Dartmoor*, J. Ll. W. Page tells of a superstitious burial practice which prevailed at Manaton in olden times, of carrying the corpse before interment three times round the cross which stood in the churchyard. There appears to be no record as to whether or not this practice had reference to the three persons of the Trinity, or that three was regarded as a magical number. The rector of the village discouraged the heathenish rite—or was it a druidical rite, for the white surplice of the priesthood is itself a remnant of some older religion—and the cross was mysteriously removed by night. Similar practices, it may be, obtained elsewhere, but Dorset, though not void of degrading superstitions in the past, possesses no record of this practice. Yet almost every village must have possessed a cross of some kind.

After the reign of Constantine the Great—whose mother, legend says, discovered the true cross buried on Calvary's Hill together with others reputed to be those on which the two thieves were hung—ornamental crosses began to spring up in public places and on public buildings. In the fourth century, Britain being still under the heel of the Roman, Constantine was in this country when his father the Emperor Constantius died at York. The influence of Constantine, whose vision of a flaming cross in the sky led to his conversion to Christianity, was possibly responsible for the inauguration of the cross as a symbol in Britain in public places. But it must be remembered that from the burial mounds of the Angles, who invaded Britain from Schleswig during the Roman era, and who probably knew little of Roman influence until they met with Cæsar a couple of centuries later, cruciform brooches have been obtained. Did the Angles, then, regard the cross as a sacred symbol before they met the Roman?

Most of the crosses of Dorset were cut not from

Purbeck or Portland, but from Hamhill stone and were, presumably, quarried under the jurisdiction of the Duchy of Cornwall. Hamhill is an abrupt eminence of oolitic formation near Yeovil. The stone obtained from its quarries is very hard and durable. The shaft of the old English cross in Puncknowle Churchyard, which is made of Hamhill stone, even now showing pittings almost microscopic in extent, is still extremely hard after five long centuries of weathering. The same might be said of many other remains, for the Dorset crosses fell in Puritan or Cromwellian times and now consist mostly of broken remains. A few have been restored. The restored cross of Corfe Mullen, in its simple dignity, is pleasant to look upon, no attempt having been made to recapture a decorated style from the past. The new cross at Shillingstone is somewhat of a departure from the praiseworthy modern idea of a cross as a symbol of dignity. One may be sure that the flaming cross which Constantine saw in the sky was free from ornament of any kind, like that other cross which was the origin of the symbol.

A bold cross of unknown age, whose origin is lost in antiquity, stands in a small plantation of pine trees by the side of the Chickerell-Abbotsbury road at the turn for Langton Herring. It is barely four feet in height and is of simple Latin design. This cross, it has been conjectured, was a call to prayer to pilgrims when travelling of old on foot between Abbotsbury and some other religious house. Only a few miles intervene between the cross and Abbotsbury, where at one time a Benedictine Abbey stood, founded in the days of Canute. A cross at such a point, for such a special purpose, suggests other crosses at similar stages of progress. No evidence seems forthcoming that such other crosses ever existed between Abbotsbury and Winchester, or even Weymouth on the coast.

In the churchyard of Rampisham, a village hidden away in the hills beyond Cattistock, there are some interesting remains of a sixteenth-century cross. This cross was an elaborate construction of the Bishops Lydeard and Stalbridge type, with an extension of the base into a preacher's platform, similar to the dole-table in the churchyard of Cheselbourne. The sides of the socket in which the cross was fixed were carved in relief, with biblical and historical figures, now much defaced. One group is said to represent the murder of Thomas à Becket, which took place more than three centuries earlier. The outlines of the figures—Peter the Apostle, Stephen the Martyr, Edmund of East Anglia, who refused to worship Odin at the command of the Dane, Thomas à Becket—may even now be traced with comparative ease if not with entire conviction.

By the side of the roadway on the lone top of Batcombe Hill, between High Stoy and Evershot, a rounded stone pillar is all that remains of Cross-and-Hand, a name somewhat redolent in style of the double-barrelled name of an inn. The stories connected with the pillar are various and uncertain. It is unlike any Christian cross in Dorset or in Somerset. The average traveller would glance at the stone and pass on unimpressed. Yet legend has woven thrilling stories about this small and negligible relic. Readers of Thomas Hardy's novels will know it as the stone on which Tess Durbeyfield laid her hand at the bidding of Alec d'Urberville, swearing, meantime, never more to tempt him. Lovers of the novelist's poems will associate the pillar with the legend of the lost pyx—lost by a priest from Cerne on a rough night, when the storm 'smote as in savage joy.' The legend is a singularly beautiful one as told in the Wessex Poems. Probably, however, the pillar by the roadside on Batcombe Hill had an origin not unconnected with the ramifications of the Roman Empire into the hill country of Dorset. A Roman road from Dorchester to Ilchester ran close by Batcombe Hill. A short rough loop road connects the two roads to-day. At Rampisham, some way west of the lone hill, there was once a Roman settlement. At Halstock there was another, with others to the north and east.

* * * * *

In passing from crosses to gargoyles one leaves the sacred for the grotesque. The original intention in the mind of man when he conceived the idea of the gargoyle was, of course, that the creature, in whatever form, should do the duty of a water spout. Its first purpose was utilitarian. Its business was to protect the outside walls of the church or tower in which it happened to be built from the slow percolation of rain-water or the more vigorous assault of storms. For this reason the mouth of the gargoyle must be as wide open as possible. A number of interesting methods of increasing the width of the mouth may be seen on the village churches of Dorset. Grotesque heads of man, or mythical beast, are presented with fingers or claws in the corners of the mouth increasing the gape by pulling sideways. The result is decidedly inelegant. It may be deemed ugly or amusing according to the mood of the onlooker. But the gargoyles are never repulsive. The best and worst that may be said of them, perhaps, is that they are grotesque, for all the agitations possible to man which are not of a peaceful kind must, one thinks, be presented in the faces of the gargoyles of Dorset.

Devon is proud that all her colours of earth, sea and sky are brought out in the beautiful Devon ware which may be bought in her shops. I do not know if Dorset has ever boasted that the scorn, anger or malice felt by her people throughout the centuries is epitomized in her gargoyles. Yet each and every young bride walking to the village church upon her wedding day, must face the grin of the gargoyle on porch, parapet or tower. When she comes out a wife the gargoyle grins behind her back as if at the perpetration of just one other hoax. The tale of 'holy matrimony' spoken within the church has escaped the ear of the gargoyle, for on the stony heads there are no asses' ears. Those organs upon the gargoyles are often but poorly developed.

The origin of the grimacing gargoyle was of very early date. It may have had its birth in the brain of some monkish head where lurked a sense of humour, or, on the other hand, the idea may have been drawn from meditation on the world of Nature and developed into sculptural art. The latter suggestion, prompted by a visit to Stogumber Church, where, near the top of the tower, a carved alligator-like reptile keeps watch over the Somerset village, is full of interest. The much-weathered Hound Tor on Dartmoor, when carefully observed, yields many an illusive head of toad or crocodile, far more substantial and realistic than faces in the fire. 'Come along,' said a friend to me one day on the moor, 'and I'll show you a huge toad's head in stone.' From Bowerman's Nose he led the way to the weathered masses of Hound Tor, where to be sure were reptile's heads enough and to spare. It would be impossible to say where the sculptor of the Stogumber gargoyle got his model. For ought that is now known it may have been the result of a mere whim, or a sincere desire to show that old enemy, the serpent, in safe custody on the church tower. The Stogumber gargoyle consists of the head of the creature, the remainder of the body being safely incorporated in the walls, and the tail neatly coiled on the western or northern side of the tower. The head and tail are visible from the street of the village below.

The gargoyles in Dorset are in various stages of dilapidation, the result of centuries of weathering. On the quiet church of Broadwindsor there is a savage-looking head with toothless jaws and cavernous eye-socket, the second eye being filled with emerald moss embrowned with microscopic cups. Time, the healer of scars and wounds has given the relic a touch of beauty. On thè church porch of Whitchurch Canonicorum, a little distance from the last-mentioned village, is a wild, bearded head, a model for some cartoonist working the period of King Charles. In the corner of the same porch below the parapet, the nearest neighbour of the bearded head for quite seven centuries, there is another head, half cat, half ogre, pulling its mouth wide open with chiselled fingers of stone. Similar types abound on churches throughout the county of Dorset. On the church tower of sequestered Sydling there are, perhaps the most grotesque figures of all. The savage head here excels in uncouthness by the adoption of little imps mounted about the ears of the gargoyle, their fingers stretching the mouth of the victim to the greatest possible extent. The gargoyle, even after so many centuries, still wears an expression of suffering, though it be only in stone.

Between the gargoyles of West Dorset and those of St. Peter's, Dorchester, with others in the Cerne Valley, there is a difference which is, perhaps, more real than apparent. One might dismiss the subject with a hasty conclusion that a similar aspect marks all the gargoyles of Dorset. But there is a dignity about the carved heads of Broadwindsor for example, not possessed by the weird animals which threaten to plunge down, upon the passer-by under the walls of St. Peter's Church, or the gargoyles already mentioned at Sydling. These creatures are grotesque in a way not simu-

GARGOYLE AT SYDLING ST. NICHOLAS

lated by the genuine water-spout which has a duty to perform. Restraint, after all, is priceless in a gargoyle as in everything else. Without it the world would become as jungle, and the sculptor's art a supercilious or a voluptuous show. There is no doubt that in past ages the religious feeling of West Dorset was dominated by the Abbey of Forde on the extreme western verge of the county. The ruling spirit there for a lifetime was one Thomas Chard, an upright man who brought the abbey to the zenith of its beauty, power, and fame. An atmosphere emanating from the seclusion and culture of the abbey threw its influence over the surrounding country, and a quiet dignity begot by that influence touched the building of the village churches. The people had begun to think of architecture in pure Gothic terms.

At the Abbey of Cerne things were not the same. The abbot held great tracts of land, and the greedy tentacles of the monastic institution reached down to the port of Christchurch in Hants, some thirty or forty miles away. Questionable actions took place there on the sea, in which an abbot of Cerne was involved, and the vast wealth of the abbey increased. The abandonment of strict integrity for the pursuit of wealth by any and every means, must have told its tale on the cowled inmates and their work and the influence they shed abroad. Gargoyles developed without restraint, and that which should have been curious or grotesque, became ugly, savage, ravenous, with the impress of the jungle, which knows neither law nor beauty. The lines quoted below from that fascinating book, *The Story of Forde Abbey*, are more applicable to Cerne than to the Abbey of Forde, for nothing remains of Cerne Abbey but a dilapidated gateway and St. Augustine's well.

> We turn to dust, and all our mightiest works
> Die too : the deep foundations that we lay
> Time ploughs them up, and not a trace remains.
> We build with what we deem eternal rock ;
> A distant age asks where the fabric stood ;
> And in the dust sifted and searched in vain
> The undiscoverable secret sleeps.

CHAPTER IX

THE EAST OF DORSET

To beat the boundaries of a county in an irresponsible fashion such as any idle wanderer may adopt is a light-hearted undertaking. With a tank full of the necessary spirit and brakes in perfect order; a sky-blue, tinted Bartholomew within the pocket of the car, one flings dull care away at the compelling moment when the green light of liberty says 'Go.' You do not halt like one with time upon his hands, you go at once. The urgent call of the open road makes nerves and sinews tingle, and mind and heart alike bound with a sense of freedom.

We shall set out from the precincts of Wimborne Minster when the little soldier in the tower comes out to strike the bells at the hour of nine. The fresh dews of early September bestrew the grass around the venerable minster with diamonds and with pearls. Some lie in clusters in open pockets spun from spiders' finest silk. Gossamers floating in the air, invisible to the eye, touch the face with the lightness of thistledown. It is a Keats' day, to-day, tranquil, as befits the 'season of mists.'

The first place of call is some six or seven miles

away, where the tower and ruins of an ancient church, draped in shining ivy, stand within the rings of a forgotten pagan temple. The place is known as Knowlton temple. While musing upon this very unusual spectacle, let us recall Pope Gregory's letter sent by the hand of a priest to St. Augustine in Britain, and recorded in Bede's *Ecclesiastical History*. 'When, therefore, Almighty God shall bring you to the most reverend Bishop Augustine, our brother, tell him what I have upon mature deliberation on the affair of the English determined upon, viz., that the temples of the idols in that nation ought not to be destroyed, but let the idols that are in them be destroyed, let holy water,' &c. At Knowlton the command of the Pope was carefully observed, for the rings even yet are unbroken, save for the temple-opening towards the east, and another towards the west, which is most probably an occupation road. Over the rough grass of the central floor of an erstwhile pagan temple, the gentle September breeze blows through twining ivy on tower and deserted nave. The round arches of the church remain, but the chancel wall and the east window have gone down before devouring time and onslaughts of wind and weather. History tells nothing of the dedication of this plot of ground, whether at first it was sacred to mighty Jupiter or to Isis, to the Genius Loci, or to Fortuna herself, whom even Christians often worship, be it only subconsciously.

Between the deserted temple church and Cranborne, the Chasetown of *Tess of the d'Urbervilles*, only a few miles intervene. At Cranborne there is a beautiful manor house whose first foundations were laid in the tenth century. Permission to see the interesting interior may, perchance, be obtained by previous application. The manor belongs to the Marquis of Salisbury. The castellated gateway of this ancient manor is a detached structure overgrown with climbing plants, and is in itself a thing of beauty. The present house is Tudor in style, and was built in the reigns of Henry VII and VIII. King John stayed here many times in an earlier building. The room in which he slept is shown to visitors. Queen Elizabeth and Charles I also stayed at Cranborne Manor House. From an airy room known as the priest's room, one descends by a spiral staircase of stone steps to a corridor, and then to the minstrel's gallery at one end of the spacious banqueting hall. A heavy door of polished oak, studded with square-headed nails, leads from the great hall to the staircase, which is of polished oak throughout.

One thing that is told in connexion with Cranborne Manor House makes too much demand on one's credulity. On a corridor of the beautiful Tudor mansion there is an old chest of carved oak. It is heavy, iron bound and polished. A tradition of the Manor says that this was the chest in which the lady of the 'mistletoe bough' lay hidden in her bridal gown. To hear this story in a century that has little to do with old romance takes one by surprise. In the late eighteenth or early nineteenth century the poet Rogers, a contemporary of Byron, wrote in blank verse and in an Italian setting, a poem entitled 'Ginevra.' The heroine of the poem was a member of the Orsini family of Modena in Italy, and the incidents of the story are precisely those of the English mistletoe-bough song. The Bridegroom of Rogers' poem was called Francesco, and the mouldering oak chest when moved 'burst and fell' revealing the skeleton of Ginevra fifty years after the death of the last of the Orsini. Between the goodly chest of Cranborne Manor House and the mouldering one of the Rogers' poem there is an irreconcilable disparity of condition.

On leaving Cranborne for Pentridge Hill, where the eastern boundary of the county is marked by the Bokerley dyke, one winds along by way of Boveridge through sylvan lanes bordering fields of yellow corn. For a mile or more the roadway runs below but parallel with the great dyke. The Bokerley dyke is thought by some to be a Romano-British earthwork. By others it is regarded as a frontier ditch excavated for defence purposes by the Saxons. It is some four miles long and stretches from Blagdon Hill on Pentridge to Vernditch on the edge of Cranborne Chase. The perpendicular earthen wall of the great chalk ditch is overgrown on Blagdon with great patches of golden ragwort. There is a fine prospect of Cranborne Chase and most of Southern Wiltshire from the top of Pentridge. The whole area as far as the eye can see teems with antiquarian interest of a most absorbing kind. Between Pentridge and Salisbury northwards, Grim's Dyke may still be traced along the hills. Near at hand, the course of the Ackling Dyke may be seen winding over Bottlebush Down from Gussage hill beyond. Below, in a corner of the fenced down, a cluster of round mounds marks the site of Worbarrow, where human remains were found of the Roman-British period, whose condition minus heads and feet gave evidence of appalling cruelty.

A narrow road runs down from the dyke on Blagdon Hill to the straggling village of Pentridge. Another trackway, a misleading will-o-the-wisp, goes over the greensward of Martin Down to the Wiltshire village of the same name. A third, which is not easily negotiable for motors, runs parallel with the Bokerly Dyke to the Roman road from Sarum, scarcely a couple of miles away. This last road should be traversed on foot. The exhilarating air of the chalk downs is amazingly tonic in quality. The romps over the Wiltshire-Dorset downs from Coombe Bissett to Tarrant Hinton and Blandford—one of the rarer pleasures of life—is only equalled by the trip from Marlborough to Devizes, from Avebury to Swindon, from Hungerford to Calne, or from Burbage over the ridgeway northwards.

On the bare chalk downs in the vicinity of the Roman road mentioned above, the boundary of the county turns definitely westwards. The downs hereabout are remarkable in September for the cheerful carpet of eyebright which covers the lower levels. About Woodyates and Handley Hill, by the side of the highway near the county boundary, thousands of the purple-veined flowers make a sort of milky way in late summer and early autumn. The tiny plant seems to cover an area where many excavations were made by the late General Pitt-Rivers, to whose devoted work as an antiquary the Farnham Museum near at hand bears witness. One shrinks from describing the exhibits taken from ancient British barrows, for the task is a too melancholy one. But the lines of skulls, exhibited on various shelves, collected from Handley Hill, Worbarrow and other parts of Cranborne Chase, claim attention on account of the preservation of teeth still fast in their natural sockets. It may be that these are the skulls of men who died young in battle. Of very considerable interest, too, are the burial urns, large and small, taken from barrows of Dorset and Wilts. These are of baked earth, dark red or brown in colour. Some are almost black with age and centuries of contact with the soil. Most have a simple form of ornamentation upon them. There are many of these British, or Romano-British urns in the Farnham Museum on Cranborne Chase.

At Handley Cross one leaves the Salisbury-Blandford highway for the less frequented byways of the Chase. The bare downs and the eyebright of Handley Hill are exchanged for wooded slopes, short cuts into deep thickets where one may expect to hear the piercing note of Pan's pipe 'blinding sweet by the river,' or by some shining pool full of blue sky and trembling leaves.

Just over the county boundary there is a pool at Tollard Royal girt about with lordly beech trees, where a charm of goldfinches may, per-

WOOL MANOR

chance, be heard and seen high up among the leaves in summer or in autumn. On the steep slope which leads up to the church there is a beech tree of majestic proportions, and another of equal size within the ancient God's acre. Tollard Royal is beautifully situated, and must have a delectable climate, since it is sheltered on the north and east by the high chalk downs of southern Wiltshire. Domesday Book makes mention of a vineyard here. A village obviously existed on the spot in very early times. There are broken memorial stones in the churchyard which were raised by families now passed from the memory of man. Others there are which have a striking resemblance in style to a Roman tombstone which has been long in the British Museum. In these old stones of Tollard Royal there remains a trace, no doubt, of Roman influence in memorials as in so many other things of a more utilitarian kind. The great numbers of prostrate figures of men and women in alabaster, marble and stone, which survive as ornate memorials of many rich families in our churches, were probably the outcome in the first place of Roman funeral ceremonial. One of these reposeful figures lies prone on a horizontal slab in the church of Tollard Royal between the pews in the centre of the building. A beautiful stained-glass window to the memory of the Honourable Alice Arbuthnot atones for this lack of true artistic sense. Immortality in stone is heavy and unconvincing, in a window, light and ethereal. A number of windows at Tollard Royal possess yellow-figured glass apparently of the same period as the amber lights of the east window of Coombe Keynes.

One looks in vain on the sills of church windows in Dorset for samples of the old slipper-shaped oil lamps which were used in Roman times. In Wool Church there is one of a more primitive type. This consists of a square stone less than a foot high, with four deep cup-shaped borings an inch and half across, each of which would be filled with oil. Drawings of the slipper-shaped lamps indicate that one or two wicks only were used in lamps approaching that shape.

Leaving Tollard Royal, the highway, as well as the eastern boundary of the county, turns towards the north-west, and a fine prospect of the chalk downs about Winklebury Camp comes immediately into view. Above the valley of the Stour the highway and the county boundary run close together over the Dorset downs towards Shaftesbury. On the way several interesting places may be observed. The first of these is Ashmore, the highest village in Dorset. To reach it one must double back on the downs along a secondary road which runs between hedges, where the vast prospect is blotted out. In Domesday Ashmore appears as Aisemare—an arresting name since it is suggestive of Aysgarth or Asgard the home of the gods of the Norsemen. The situation of Aisemare is less savage than the setting of Aysgarth. As a rendezvous for the Ases—the Nature gods of the Norsemen—it leaves nothing to be desired. It has no gaping watery chasm to suggest the Norseman's Ginnungagap, with its welter of chaos and misery. But the deep, waterless hollows of the chalk downs, whose bottoms in mid-winter are scarcely touched by refreshing sunlight, are full of the great, rounded shadows of the shoulders of the hills. When the weak, winter sunlight comes aslant the hills, the great shadows darken and blacken and take on a monitory or even a menacing aspect, beside which the deafening rattle of thunder in summer is exhilarating to the spirit. The chalk downs, can indeed, be lonely in the extreme.

A zealous philologist may see in Aisemare some trace of a Celtic word for water, as in the river Aisne in France. There is a great pool in the midst of the village, the dew-ponds on the downs, and a well here and there. And that is all. When Domesday was compiled Ashmore was more important than it is to-day. The meeting of the Hundred Court was held on the downs near one of the ancient barrows in the parish of Ashmore, and on the hills above Fontmell Magna, where one barrow at least is still to be seen, strange sounds used to be heard in olden times, and probably may still be heard. This vocal demonstration on the down in the quiet of evening had nothing to do with so-called singing barrows. It was believed that the creatures responsible for the sounds were of the air and not of the earth. They were called gappergennies, but of what species or genus, or whether bird-like, bat-like, or merely spectral no explanation seems forthcoming. The sounds, it has been suggested, were made by badgers which live upon the ground, but whether or no these creatures have a ventriloquial power is not made apparent. A robin redbreast certainly may have that peculiar power. At Anstey's Cove, in Devonshire, I heard a redbreast which, while standing on a table, projected its voice to the roof of a shed with mystifying results. It seemed to compress the throat by turning the point of the half-closed beak very stiffly upwards, towards the roof, from which the voice returned. There is a school for children at Ashmore first opened by a member of the Society of Friends a century and a half ago. There can be little doubt that under the enlightening influence of education the gappergennies have unfortunately disappeared.

From Ashmore the county boundary and the highway run together to a point where the Ox Drove crosses the road at the top of Charlton and Melbury Downs. The green trackway known as the Ox Drove is a hollow worn down during long ages by the passage of ox-teams, from Winklebury Camp, a Celtic earthwork in Wiltshire, to some other place. Where the teams were bound for exactly it would be impossible to say. The Drove is said to trail along the downs towards Compton Abbas. From the point where it crosses the road on the high land, whose jutting spurs form Charlton and Melbury Downs, it is perceptible along the hill tops as a ribbon of rough trackway towards Winklebury four miles eastward. There is another arm of the deep track running below the road to Shaftesbury, on the slope of Charlton Down. Here again, as at Handley Hill, are numberless plants of eyebright strewn on the steep hillside among gentians, equally plentiful. On the top of Zig-Zag Hill, as the lower part of Charlton Down is called, the boundary glances off northwestwards round Shaftesbury. The road on Zig-Zag Hill has several sharp hairpin bends, hence the name. By taking this tricky road one keeps just within the county boundary. From this point Shaftesbury is quickly gained. It is not an everyday experience to descend on Shaston. Usually one climbs a steep hill to the old town perched aloft above the valley of the Stour.

The glory of Shaftesbury, in the first hey-day of its pride, was the abbey which Alfred built. Even now, antiquarians, by excavating on the site of the abbey are trying to recapture that glory. History seems almost mute on the subject of this religious house. Aethelgiva, the daughter of King Alfred, was the first abbess there. At a later date, Goda, sister of Edward the Confessor, was also head of the abbey at Shaftesbury. Of the latter abbess, Goda, in her capacity as landowner at the abbey, Domesday makes mention several times. The abbey of Shaftesbury was in possession of upwards of forty-five square miles of territory in various parts of the county. The many hides of land, Saxon measure, which go to make up a territory of thirty thousand acres, were distributed over areas as wide apart as Handley on Cranborne Chase, Compton Abbas in the Stour valley, and Corfe Castle in Purbeck. Before Domesday was compiled the king had purchased a hide of land within the manor estates of Kingston, then belonging to the abbey of Shaftesbury, in order to regain the site of Corfe Castle, which was originally built by the Saxon King Edgar during the tenth century. In exchange for the hide of land the king gave to the abbess the advowson of Gillingham Church.

The north-east corner of Dorset, of which Gillingham is the geographical centre, with Shaftesbury five miles to the southwards towards Cranborne Chase, is full of historical interest. Edward the Confessor was proclaimed king at Gillingham in 1042 at a gathering of the Witan. This must have been one of the latest assemblies of the English parliament before the coming of William of Normandy. The spot where the historic gathering took place is some two hundred yards from the present road to Shaftesbury. It is marked by raised banks, the remnants of the foundations of a palace. The remains of a moat may be traced in wet weather, when pools of water lie in the grass-grown ditch. Within the boundary of the banks and the ditch, ruminating cows now sleep on a summer afternoon.

North of Gillingham, just over the county boundary amid lovely scenery, is the wooded ridge of Penselwood. It was here that Edmund Ironside defeated Cnut, and drove him out of Wessex. Yet Cnut, the Dane, lived to be king of all England, including Wessex, and died at Shaftesbury. He was buried at Winchester, his remains even now occupying a chest within the great cathedral.

Chapter X

A WRITER OF RURAL VERSE

MANY are the uses of poetry. The man who, escaping from the world of business, can listen with delight to the click of stirrups and clanking of armour in 'Marmion,' 'Rokeby,' and 'The Lord of the Isles,' has justified the 'big, bow-bow strain' in the work of Sir Walter Scott. Flowers of speech he will find by the way as well as flowers of the field, while the bugle rings distantly in his ears.

National feeling will be awakened in every poem, at many stages of progress and on numerous pages of rhyming verse.

> Breathes there the man with soul so dead,
> Who never to himself hath said
> This is my own, my native land!
> Whose heart hath ne'er within him burned,
> As home his footsteps he hath turned,
> From wandering on a foreign strand!

William Wordsworth's mode of expression was in a different strain. A few of his earlier poems are somewhat akin to the rural verses of the Dorset poet, the Rev. William Barnes. Both the Dorset and the Cumberland poets were serious-minded men, and though the Dorset poet would never have written :

> Our birth is but a sleep and a forgetting ;
> The soul that rises with us, our life's star
> Hath had elsewhere its setting,
> And cometh from afar ;

he yet did write, 'The Geäte a-Vallèn to.' Each of the poems just mentioned touches the fringe of the great uncertainties, the one with a tenderness that moves us all, the other with the strength and insight of divine philosophy. The 'six years darling of a pigmy size' whose 'whole vocation' is 'endless imitation,' is only one in the great succession of wearers of the 'little shoe' behind which love can ever hear 'the geäte a-vallèn to.' The Cumberland poet tells the story of the child's growth to manhood and mature thought in a great Ode, the Dorset poet in forty lines of musical verse. There is no intent of comparing the two aspects, in bringing the poems together, for they are not comparable. One's head demands the Ode for intellectual satisfaction, and the straightening out of tangled thought, after the heart has taken comfort from the Dorset poet's tender verse :

> And Oh ! it is a touchen thing
> The loven heart must rue
> To hear behind his last farewell
> The geäte a-vallen to.

In 'Readen ov a Headstowne,' a poem similar in association to the Cumberland poet's 'We are seven,' a family history is revealed in thirty-two lines of fluent verse. The poet Barnes was reading an inscription on a tombstone when a child ran up and pushed aside 'a bunch o' bennets' that were covering a verse cut upon the stone. It does not appear whether the word 'bennets' indicates bent grass or the yellow-flowered herb bennet, the Herba Benedicta of the monasteries. But as bennets are mentioned in other poems, it is possible that the poet refers to bent grass, in spite of the alleged potency of herb-bennet as a safeguard where spiritual matters are concerned. The picture one's mind conjures up of the child's ingenuous expression, as she holds the bennets aside, and reveals the lines inscribed to her mother's memory is more realistic than the voice of the maiden, who reiterated 'We are seven.' We can hear the voice of the Dorset maiden who 'bides at Betty White's o' t'other zide o' road,' and see the movement of the little slender arm as she pushes the bennets away. She is a pathetic, orphaned creature, as sweet and innocent a figure as any in the literature of the county of Dorset.

From the poem on Poll, 'The Milkmaid o' the Farm,' there emanates an atmosphere akin to that of Talbothayes, with its bevy of milkmaids, the emasculate Angel Clare, and the rhythmic sound of milk spurting into deep cans. One sees the sparkling eyes, the red cheeks, the stately tread of the milkmaid's walk, and believes her to be indeed as happy 'as if she wore a goolden crown.' But Poll, like the milkmaids of Talbothayes is too abundantly corporeal. One can see that in spite of the rhyme and music of the verse, and the poet's fascination at the sight of rural happiness. A thoroughbred Saxon was Poll undoubtedly, whose 'yollow cream' and butter, and 'cheeses red an' white,' lesser women may long to enjoy. Like Alice in Wonderland the average woman would need the telescopic power of shutting herself up in the presence of the buxom maiden, whose face is her fortune, and whose physique is her finest asset. Face to face with her own kind of more gentle upbringing, the womanhood of the milkmaid may seem relentless autocracy. For sheer physical strength the odds are all on her side.

One would have liked Poll better with a song upon her lips instead of the proverbial cherries. Perhaps that is why 'The Milkmaid o' the Farm' reminds one of Wordsworth's solitary reaper :

> Alone, she cuts and binds the grain,
> And sings a melancholy strain ;
> Oh ! listen ! for the vale profound
> Is overflowing with the sound.
>
> * * * * * *
>
> Will no one tell me what she sings ?
> Perhaps the plaintive numbers flow
> For old, unhappy, far-off things,
> And battles long ago.

The solitary reaper is a great contrast to the red-cheeked Poll, though dependent on the land in much the same way. She is a Celt endowed—or burdened, as you will—with Celtic melancholy.

In possession of race memory she 'is moved to fill the vale profound' with a strain in keeping with the deep valley and the reverberating echo among the hills. She is at once beautiful as a sentient being, illusive as a spiritual one, a vital, pulsating link between a past age and a future. These are the things which appeal to the higher moments of our being. But it is the nature of humankind to be attracted by a different set of facts and to sing with increasing ardour :

> Take a pair of sparkling eyes
> And a pair of ruby lips.

In the poem 'Blackmwore Maidens,' the Dorset poet described that which he knew well, for Blackmoor vale was his native heath. He was born in 1801 at Rushay Farm, near Sturminster Newton, by the side of the tributary Lydden, ere that stream is joined by the Caundle Brook. These two streams are cradled in the region of Giant Head Hill and High Stoy, respectively. From either one, or both of the hills, the traveller going northward descends into the country of The Woodlanders and Giles Winterborne of fragrant memory. It is a peaceful countryside, about which there winds one of the loveliest and most secluded lanes in the county. How fair the valley of the Stour and its tributary streams may be, none can know who has not seen it in the spring o' the year.

> The primwrose in the sheade do blow
> The cowslip in the zun,
> The thyme upon the down do grow,

The clote where streams do run ;
An' where do pretty maidens grow
An' blow, but where the tow'r
Do rise among the 'bricken tuns,'
In Blackmwore by the Stour.

When visiting the 'bricken tuns,' or villages of Blackmoor vale, one looks involuntarily for the chestnut hair of the adorable Marty South. Marty's sale of her beautiful hair will be remembered by all readers of the 'Woodlanders.' But the colour is rare even among the pretty maidens of the Stour valley. Casual observations in and about the borders of the neighbouring counties, would seem to show that chestnut-haired maidens are more frequently seen over the Somerset border. The Rev. William Barnes tells us nothing of the colour of Blackmoor maidens' hair, though he observed their dainty way of 'steppen off the stiles.'

It was the Dorset poet's ambition, we are told, to present his poems in Anglo-Saxon words. From this point of view they are an interesting study, though many words used had their origin in Frisian, Icelandic, and Norse. Perhaps these, being North European, distinct from the Latin tongue, were regarded as Anglo-Saxon in origin. But, even so, words of French derivation, such as dower and bachelor, were required even in the construction of Blackmoor maidens. If we take into consideration the names of most of our hills, rivers and headlands it would be easy to confront our Anglo-Saxon enthusiasts with a bewildering list of Anglo-Celtic origin, which, by virtue of lineage from the original possessors of the soil, would make the Anglo-Saxon tongue appear an intrusion of modern date. The name of Dorset itself, is derived from the Celtic dwr-water, which root is present in almost its original form in the name of Durotriges. Pen, as in Pilsdon Pen, is well known as a common Celtic name of many a hill and headland of the west coast of England. I am told that an unsolicited pension from the Civil List was allotted to the poet as an acknowledgement of his eminence as a philologist. There is one poem, however, which unconsciously reveals his worth in a calling more intimate to his personality than the construction of a philological treatise. That poem is 'Vo'k a'comen into Church.' In that brief poetical utterance the sympathetic care of the shepherd for his flock proves the deep and earnest nature of the faithful pastor. The Rev. William Barnes as a priest in holy orders was greater, after all, than the philologist who dwelt in the rectory of Winterborne Came.

Speech is a living thing which develops by easy stages like every creature that breathes the breath of life. To render the language of our nation purely Saxon, would be to sterilize its productivity, distort and dwarf its structure like the binding of Chinese feet. The Dorset writer of rural verse wrote some three hundred and fifty poems of varied quality, many of them perfect works of art. Even now, some forty odd years after the poet's death, one would barter much of the philological research for another score of poems comparable to 'The Guide-Post,' 'The

Slanten Light o' Fall,' or 'The Geäte a-Vallên to,' all written, without reserve, in the dialect of the county. Had the poet's heart been undivided these might have come into being.

Among the most pleasing of the descriptive poems are those which describe the movements of Dorset maidens engaged in their regular occupations about the village street or the countryside. There is the maiden who laughs in 'To Me,' and sweet Jessie who listens in 'Two an' Two.' We know that Jessie is sweet, or the poet could not have unburdened himself in those beautiful pictures of scenes all the people of Dorset know—the corn 'a-weaven down below'—the grass wearing dewy beads—cattle in the shade of the trees.

A succession of bewitching maidens 'gawin down the steps for water,' conjured up by the poem bearing that title is another case in point. The village spring of sparkling water is the meeting place where the swain in the poem first saw the maiden who later becomes his bride. On seeing the wedding guests pass down the village street the poet resolves :

> An' if I've luck, I woont be slow
> To teake off woone that I do know,
> A-trippen gaily to an' fro,
>   Upon the steps for water.

There is here a picture akin to that of Blackmoor Maiden 'steppen off the stiles.' The graceful movements of buoyant youth, the quick, unerring motion of slender limbs is viewed, apparently, as the poetry of motion, something so beautiful in itself that the eye dwells on it lingeringly.

Another poem which is as beautiful for association as the foregoing is 'The Slanten Light o' Fall.' The incident of this poem is an autumn christening, recalled in homely language on the wedding-day of the infant, now grown to womanhood. The stream of light which broke through the clouds and shone on the tiny infant was 'The Slanten Light o' Fall.' It is autumn again, and the same October light shines upon the bride as she leaves the church which long ago saw her christening and now has witnessed her marriage.

Two other poems on the Fall—'Corn a'turnin' Yollow' and 'A-haulen o' the Corn'—are descriptive of the beauty of southern cornfields in autumn. The figure of Jeane, with a garland of red poppies about her head, gives one more pleasing portrait of a Dorset maiden, and Cousin Poll who turns up unexpectedly in apple orchard or country lane, is the lively Puck of the poems. Then there is 'Milken Time,' 'The Leane,' and 'The Zummer Hedge,' all minutely descriptive of homely or pastoral scenes. 'Tokens' is an interesting poem of another kind which, along with 'I'm out o' Doors,' gives one some insight of the poet's keen powers of observation.

One gets back to quiet meditation in that beautiful poem, 'The Turn o' the Days,' as well as in 'The Guide Post,' which, in the poet's hands, becomes endowed with life. Here, indeed is a stroke of genius. The delight of personal possession shines out from 'I Got Two Vields,' and the wider possession free to all sentient beings may be felt in 'Be'me'ster.' The bells of Lydlinch Church, throwing melody far and wide over the region watered by the Lydden and the Caundle brook, belong to all who may hear them. So, too, does the 'sweet bells' dyen soun'' among the hills round Beaminster.

The Christmas dinner at Herrenstone, and that other feast which gave us the verses entitled 'Don't Ceare,' will long remain two memorable Dorset meals.

There are two more girlish figures in the poet's work which catch one's imagination—'Ruth a-riden,' a girl in opulent circumstances, whose name gives the refrain for half-a-dozen verses bearing that title, and the elusive figure wearing a scarlet cloak in 'The Bwoat.' One suspects that the latter is none other than Jeane o' Grenley Mill. She is with her brother in a boat on the river Stour:

> As steätely as a queen o' vo'k,
> She zot wi' floaten scarlet cloak,
> An' commen on, at ev'ry stroke,
> Between my withy-sheaded shores.
> The broken stream did idly try
> To show her sheape a-riden by,
> The rushes brown-bloom'd stems did ply,
> As if they bow'd to her by will.

There is melancholy of a deep yet exquisite kind in 'The Bwoat'—melancholy which reminds one of Lucy who 'dwelt beside the springs of

Dove,' and of the poet Wordsworth who called his vanished love to mind with such affectionate remembrance.

* * * * *

> Lastly, came Winter, clothed all in frieze,
> Chattering his teeth for cold that did him chill.
>
> —SPENSER.

In 'The Settle an' the Girt Wood Vier' the poet of Blackmoor Vale gives a glimpse of the interior of a Dorset homestead in winter. It is such an interior as that of the colonial roadside inn, with its fire of blazing wood, described by Longfellow in 'Tales of a Wayside Inn.' Any one conversant with American poetry will recall 'The Red Horse,' and the stories that were there told. The music of the verses on the spacious hearth lies in the Dorset poet's refrain:

> Ah! gi'e me, if I were a squier,
> The settle an' the girt wood vier.

This is the burden of the poem, which is, I believe, a general favourite with Dorset people. Apart from the musical refrain, the poem is a denunciation of new household ways, of small fireplaces and the many minor things which make for modern comfort. It harks back to old usages, when the bacon flitch hung in the chimney nook, and the twanging wires of the rude humstrum were heard at Christmastide.

After a careful study of any particular author, it is interesting to look back and consider how one came to be drawn to such a pursuit, whether it be in pursuance of art, literature, or religion—if one may chance to have any claim to the last. My answer to the query as far as regards the Dorset dialect poet is easy indeed. I was driving quickly through the streets of Dorchester some fourteen years ago when my eye alighted for one brief minute on a bronze statue outside St. Peter's Church. The poetry, yea, even the name of the Rev. William Barnes was then unknown to me, but my erring mind saw some impossible similarity to a figure I had long known in the market place of Uttoxeter. But that a statue of Samuel Johnson should be here in the south I knew to be improbable. I returned immediately from the avenue along which Lucetta walked, to Dorchester, and to the statue. I made inquiries, said 'Here was a man, anyway,' and went on my journey to Cornwall. Asking later for the poems at several booksellers' shops in the county, I was told they were out of print. At length a volume was forthcoming. I read and re-read the poems, without any inclination to compare them with any other poet's work. Such comparison is needless and undesirable, for the poetic utterances of the Rev. William Barnes can stand very well by themselves. No other poet is like him. Bagber was visited, and Herringstone, with Winterborne Came, where the poet lies buried in the churchyard. At the last-mentioned place one's mind wandered off to Grasmere, to a simple stone and a well-kept grave by the Rothay. In the past I had often done homage there among the hills of Cumberland.

But here, in Dorset, the chief memorial is the statue by St. Peter's Church, standing there so full of thought close by the busy highway—a statue so void of falsity that an arrested traveller may halt betimes on her way to search out the root of the matter, where manhood is so apparent even through the hardness of bronze.

CHAPTER XI

PLANTS OF THE HEATH

LOVERS of Thomas Hardy who know *The Return of the Native,* that masterpiece of the great novelist, will be aware that Dorset contains a vast expanse of heathland, known in that novel by the name of Egdon Heath. Nowhere in these islands is bell-heather of a more deep or brilliant purple, and rarely are there so many bells in a cluster as one finds on this untameable heath. The white and grey flints of which the floor of the heath is composed throw an added depth of tint upon the empurplement of the moor. The writer knows the tint of heather in the Isle of Man, and the Lake Country, in Scotland and in Wales, on Dartmoor, Exmoor and the Mendips, but the bell-heather of Egdon Heath, in its flinty environment, surpasses any of these. With a lowering sky, such as may canopy the heath on a day of uncertain weather in August, the tints of the landscape defy description.

Of the several kinds of heather which grow upon Egdon Heath, bell or fine-leaved heather is the most vividly purple and most frequent on the higher parts of the heath. The common ling grows intermingled with it almost everywhere. The dense clusters of small pink flowers of ling are the most beautiful of all our heather flowers when seen singly under a lens, scarcely excepting even the lovely flowers of the Cornish heather. The four-leaved bog-heather is also frequent on the heath on damp ground, and the pale waxy bells of this species appear the most delicate flowers on the heath. As the heath tends to become drier in places, bog heather gives place to fine-leaved heather and ling. When the ground begins to dry, where bog heather is growing, it will be seen that the soil is black and peaty, with but little flinty admixture. On wild Stoborough Common, a part of the great heathland some dozen miles south-east of Rainbarrow and Hardy's Egdon Heath, the fringed heather is to be found with beautiful, luxurious spikes of rose pink flowers. A variety, apparently a hybrid between the pale pink bog-heather and the fringed heath grows in the same locality. When the sun shines upon them, these plants are exquisitely beautiful in their natural setting.

The broad-leaved, as well as the marsh Epipactis, commonly called helleborines, were still growing upon the heath a few years ago in places indicated in the county 'Flora.' The seeds of these plants are small as dust and are apparently without form. When mixed together with seeds of bee orchis I found it impossible to distinguish the one from the other. Both belong to the orchid family. The flowers of Epipactis are green and much less specialized than those of the bee orchis, but both in their natural haunts seed freely.

The productivity of wild plants is very interesting. The wild hyacinth or bluebell, the greygle, or graegle of Dorset, and Scilla nutans of the botanist, grows abundantly on the heath and often yields a high percentage of full capsules. Many stems in the month of June will bear twelve or fourteen capsules full of the polished, black seeds. The seeds are attractive objects, as they lie in the bleached and bursting capsules, unspilled even in late September in quiet places on the heath. Almost every one is interested in those peculiar plants, the sundews. Known botanically as species of Drosera, even a hardened botanist rarely passes them without attention. They are usually sought on boggy hill-tops, where sphagnum moss makes pale cushions of soppy verdure sprinkled, often, with the vivid yellow flowers and crimson stems of the bog asphodel. The veriest child, if allowed to run wild for a day on the slightly elevated heathlands of Dorset, would return home to give a glowing account of the red spots spread thickly over the ground round pools or in damp hollows. Plants of the round-leaved sundew may be counted by hundreds in a space of twenty square yards clinging rosette-like to the ground, while the intermediate long-leaved form is even more profuse. In the treacherous ground about the Morden decoy pool it grows along with the sky-blue gentian, G. pneumonanthe. On the verge of the pool, too, are great quantities of sweet gale bearing fat, yellowish-green catkins in autumn which fill the air with aromatic fragrance.

The composition of the top stratum of the heath, described, I believe, as Bagshot sand, is such that it can scarcely be called soil, for it is made up of minute angular fragments of quartz or flint ground up as fine as dust. My lens reveals no admixture save small fragments of limestone. On this formation, so void of nitrogenous matter, the sundew contrives to eke out an abundant life as to numbers. It is well known that these plants provide themselves with nitrogen from the small insects which alight upon the leaves, and are absorbed by the sticky secretion upon them. The leaf closes over the insect to open again when the prisoner has been digested, as it were. The stimulus which brings the leaves into action appears to be chemical as well as mechanical. Spicules of quartz or flint thrown upon the leaves by force of raindrops do not stimulate the leaves to action. Neither do raindrops. But a drop of albumen, or any nitrogenous compound in solution, excites the movement of the leaves in the same way as a fly or other insect. The law and order which pervades all Nature is here revealed in a perplexing way, for plants of sundew can support themselves without the nitrogen collected through the leaves. Experiments, made by Darwin have proved that the flowering spike is finer, and the weight of seed greater when the plant is so nourished. The seeds under the lens resemble a very short, fine hair with a small valve in the centre, and are scarcely a millimetre in length. Here, in the seed, one finds the strictly kept secret of a species or of a genus of plants. The seeds of the bog asphodel, similar in construction to those of the sundew, have a single hair fine as gossamer extending from each end of the almost microscopic valve. The valve is in the middle, but is larger and the hairs are longer than those of the sundew. The hairs are intended, it is said, to catch the wind. Both the bog asphodel and the sundew seeds, though adapted for dispersion by wind, may also secure anchorage in the slow-moving waters of the bog, through the arrest of the protruding hairs against other bog plants.

Out on the Piddle and the Froom, or Frome, two rivers which pursue a winding, spreading course over the heath — one rising north, one south of Rainbarrow—the water ranunculus flourishes all through the season. In autumn much of the submerged and floating foliage is cut or dragged away by water-hooks and left to decay. Both the Froom and the Piddle, especially the former, are slow meandering rivers, whose quiet currents give opportunity for the water ranunculus to develop great numbers of strong stems many yards in length. These are crowded with myriads of submerged, thread-like leaves. On the river at Wool Manor the foliage and white flowers of the ranunculus cover the surface of the water. The floating carpet of green spangled with white stars tempts the pied wagtails to alight. Walking apparently like Peter on the water they dart quickly to and fro on the floating leaves after the insects which form their food. Below the old six-arched bridge, the plants stretch right across the river in some seasons, a distance of some hundred feet. From the recesses on the bridge formed by the piers, little shoals of trout

BERE HEATH

from ten to twenty in number, may be seen sporting in the channels of translucent water between the floating beds of ranunculus.

> O' small-feac'd flow'r that now dost bloom
> To stud wi' white the shallow Frome,

wrote the poet Barnes, but here at Woolbridge the 'Frome' is deep, not shallow, and stems of the ranunculus are very long. Higher up the river where one creeping arm of the broad stream first enters the heathland near Woodsford, the water is shallow, and a different type of water-crowfoot almost chokes the stream. The water ranunculus runs into many forms by variation in the shape of leaf and in size of flower. Botanists recognize some fourteen species. One has an ivy-shaped leaf, another a fan-shaped leaf, a third has peltate foliage, a fourth a three-lobed leaf. A fifth may have all hair-like leaves and a sixth both thread-like and orbicular leaves.

At Dorchester the Froom is deep, and the white stars of the ranunculus sail the placid stream by the thousand with a slight dancing motion. But above the county town, at the villages of Frampton and Maiden Newton, the ranunculus is less persistent. One must follow another valley and a stream other than the Froom to trace the plant to its beginnings, to wit, the sluggish Sydling water. The valley down which this quiet stream flows is narrow, and a sequestered haunt of the kingfisher. It is the vale of Up-Sydling and Sydling St. Nicholas. The former is snugly tucked away in a corner of the hills at the foot of Batcombe Down, on the southern side. Sydling water rises in the great down, and even at Up-Sydling it is literally choked with the abundant foliage of the star-spangled water ranunculus. Seeds innumerable float downstream from the source at Up-Sydling, and deposit themselves along the course of the river Froom which Sydling water joins. Another stream which may contribute to the abundance of the ranunculus in the Froom on the heath, is the Winterburn, which flows through the several Winterbornes and from thence under Maiden Castle. In its translucent course through the villages it is dotted with white flowers for six months of the year.

Among the plants in the treacherous bogs of the southern parts of the heathlands of Dorset, one may find the two quaint skullcaps. Their value consists not in any beauty that either of the two species may possess, but is vested in a certain quaintness and comparative rarity. The upright marsh lousewort, gay with pink flowers and foliage finely cut, is at once more attractive in the bog and more plentiful than the skullcaps. Few people who are not botanists would take any notice of the latter plants, but the lousewort, in spite of its name, is attractive long after the pink flowers have fallen, for the ripe capsules, full to bursting inside the fringed calyces, are a distinctive feature of the bog wherever the plant grows.

One word more must be said for the skullcap. In a great bed of reeds mixed with sparganium, at sea level, far down Start Bay in Devon, I have seen shapely plants of the skullcap with bright blue flowers. Contrasted with the severity of the burrs and sharp green blades of sparganium, the blue of the skullcap gave character to a bed of reeds otherwise negligible both in colour and form.

Other interesting bog plants there are on the heaths of Dorset, such as the spurred, pale-flowered pinguicala commonly known as butterwort; thread-like, floating bladderwort with small yellow flowers also slightly spurred; and the hairy, or rather woolly St. John's wort, Hypericum elodes. Two quaint plants of boldly differing type are the marsh pennywort and the arrowhead. The former spreads its disc-like green leaves, which are of the size and shape of a halfpenny, on the surface of the bog. The clusters of tiny flowers are found hidden under the round leaves.

The marsh willowherb, Epilobium tetragonum, when the long capsules are full of feathery seeds, seems a strange inhabitant for a bog since the seeds of most bog plants are spilled on the ground surrounding them, which is the natural habitat of such plants. The exceptionally long pods of the marsh willowherb insure a wide dispersion of seed beyond the confines of the bog, by means of the feathery parachutes which sail away like thistledown on the wings of the wind.

In Dorset the stately arrowhead often gives an especial charm to the rivers. Its name is descriptive of the aerial leaves which rise on long stems from the bed of the river. When they reach the surface of the water these leaves slowly expand like the heads of so many arrows. The form of the leaves is very distinctive. A number of the submerged leaves shaped like blades of grass, spring from the root but remain under water. Flowering spikes mingle with the arrow-shaped leaves above the water, and each white flower is as large as a primrose. The petals are three in number, and at the base of each one there is a blotch of deep violet. This beautiful plant grows on Wareham heath and some other of the Dorset heaths.

Wool heath is separated from Moreton heath on the west by the Froom. The river flows in several channels through meadows between the two botanical treasure-grounds. Though Wool heath is not certainly richer in rareties of the plant world, it is yet, perhaps more approachable than Moreton heath because it is less intruded upon by private ownership. To the east Wool heath slopes down to the vale of the Piddle, a river as interesting in its course as it is unimaginative in name. Beyond this river is the extensive heath which from its proximity to Wareham takes the name of that town. The air of Wareham heath in summer is full of the perfume of heather, and the aromatic fragrance of sweet gale makes a pleasance of the marshy places. The golden-green or amber-like catkins of the latter plant, dotted with yellow, resinous globules, impregnate the surrounding atmosphere with a piney perfume. After the plant is gathered the fragrant scent continues to be given off for half the winter season. Globules of the yellow resinous substance are sprinkled over the leaves rendering the tiny shrub a perennial source of fragrance.

From Wareham heath and Stoborough heath the ground gains in altitude until it culminates abruptly in the steep hills of Purbeck which overlook the heathlands. On the heaths at the base of the Purbeck Hills—Creech, Grange and Povington heaths—there are many plants of botanical interest. One of the least of these is the low-growing Viola lactea, a sweet white violet with the habit of Polygala depressa. Here, too, in autumn, in the meadows of Creech Grange, one may see the lilac flowers of Colchicum or meadow saffron dotted about the grass. This is a plant of character. There are no leaves at the time of flowering. In spring they appear nursing the green capsules. The ovary is a few inches below ground down in the soil. The stemless flower rises from the ovary or bulb by means of the long, pale lilac tube. The styles which are contained within the long tube are five or six inches long—a very unusual thing in British plants—and protrude above the campanulate limb. The stamens are fixed on short stalks on the petals at the mouth of the tube. This interesting plant dots the greensward in autumn in Lady Ilchester's beautifully-wooded grounds at Melbury Park, in the hill country near Evershot.

The pyramidal orchis, so called on account of the form of the flower clusters, is common among grass in the neighbourhood of the Purbeck hills.

It is a plant of chalk and limestone soils. This orchis is of a bright rose colour and is usually sweet-scented, howbeit sometimes but slightly. It is more regular in the structure of the flowers and more uniform in colour than any other of our British orchises. On chalk and limestone soils it is as common as the spotted orchis is usually found to be on almost any soil. The latter, like the bee orchis, varies in depth of colour and in size and shape of pink, helio, or purple blotches on the variously-shaped petals. The uniformity of the pyramid orchis is one of its especial charms. The spotted orchis will be found busy swelling its seed pods by the sides of sequestered lanes, before the bright rose colour of the pyramid orchis appears among the grass.

The seeds of all species of orchis are extremely small. Calculations have been made that many millions of them would be required to make a pound in weight, yet such microscopic seeds are invested with beauty of form in the outer membranous covering. It is possible to enter into many of the small secrets of Nature without a microscope. Seeds of cranesbill got from field or hedgerow examined under a lens will reveal an outer membrane reticulated with geometrical exactness. Small brown seeds, collected from withered stalks on an estuarine mud-flat may be found, perchance, to be trimmed around with semi-transparent frills intended to give buoyancy when the seeds are launched upon the water. Wonders will be found in the scrutiny of seeds for a hundred times and in a hundred different ways, many of them probably illustrating pre-vision connected with germination:

> So careful of the type she seems,
> So careless of the single life.

A plant of Equisetum or horsetail taken from broken ground or marsh and shaken by hand when the cones are ripe, will send forth a cloud of spores which, singly, are invisible. A single spore under a lens in warm sunshine may be seen to uncurl its four feelers and spread them out as if about to start upon a journey. And so it is. The spore must have water or it will quickly perish. It contains much chlorophyll. It has been conjectured that only two spores per million have the good luck to survive and fulfil their function. The fatalities in orchis seeds may be as numerous as the casualties of horsetail spores. By how slender a thread then, hangs the survival of many a plant of pyramidal orchis, whose bright rose tint enlivens alike the succulent grasses of pasture land, and the dry false bromus of the steeply sloping ridge.

CHAPTER XII

DORSET POETRY

THE poetry of Dorset, of her landscapes, villages, brooks and ruins has not yet been written. Thomas Hardy has given us 'Pale Beech and Pine so Blue,' a pure gem from the woodlands, and 'Wessex Heights,' a golden tribute from the hills. The Rev. William Crowe, one-time rector of Stoke Abbott, loved shaggy Lewesdon and wrote a poem in its praise. Besides and apart from these and many poems of similar type, the poetry of Dorset is invested first of all with an abounding human interest. No great body of poetry in praise of Dorset shorn of the human element is in existence. There is nothing in her literature comparable to the sonnets on the Duddon for vehement love of Nature and of ruin, rock and river. No elegy that may be applied to lost humankind in every county has been written in any one of her many crowded graveyards. It may, perchance, be said that the elegy written at Stoke Poges has done that reverent service for England once for all—that no better eulogy of our long-gone English dead is likely to be written. Elegies demand great expenditure of thought and of mental energy, it may be presumed.

But Dorset is equally poor in sonnets, and these make less demand on mental energy as well as on emotion. Fine miniatures of artistic sense and finish, they are often exquisitely beautiful. A form of poetry used by Shakespeare sentimentally, by Wordsworth and Keats artistically, with such splendid results in all, might for a hundred times have clinched the entrancing grip of some bit of Dorset scenery.

Where is the poet who should have described—if only with one half of the vehement love of Wordsworth for Long Meg and her daughters—the scene around the circle of stones on the down to the south of Poxwell? Of diameter sufficient to enclose the sacrificial fire, what did this little ring witness in its tragic day, what dances, rites or orgies practised in the clear air of the dew-wet down? The spired church of Poxwell, with its windows of coloured glass, the tall trees around it made vocal by a hundred rooks, the bare, rolling downs emerald even in late November, how peaceful are they now compared with the weird picture conjured up by thoughts of pagan fires. What a sonnet this scene should have inspired with Portland Isle across the bay in the background! It would be well that our people should know and remember these things, lest one day we slip back into pagan ways. It has been said that human nature does not become retrograde on a colossal scale. How was it, then, with Carthage, with Rome, and the ancient civilizations of Central and of South America?

A sonnet of quiet reflection our unborn poet

should have written on the old church of sequestered Compton Valence, hidden in a hollow of the chalk hills hard by a Roman road. Dedicated to Thomas à Becket, distinguished by an apsidal chancel, battlemented and lichen-spotted, among fields which in summer are full of daisies and buttercups—here is inspiration for a rural sonnet charged with history and tradition. West Fleet has her 'Chapel lurking among trees,' where a few 'villagers on bended knees find solace,' each answering in its way to a Wordsworthian sonnet written long ago, on England's village churches.

Quaintly named Affpuddle, which had unworthy association with the arrest of the Tolpuddle martyrs[1] should, ere now, have figured in an ode full of fiery indignation. The Rev. William Barnes, who lived through the years of transportation of Loveless and his friends, seems never to have been moved to frenzy, such as a poet might be expected to feel at the wickedness of that unholy plot. Affpuddle on the heath unfortunately nurtured the infamous man who, by becoming informer, betrayed innocent men.

But one beautiful sonnet did have origin on the Dorset coast through the influence of Dorset scenery. When John Keats set out on his last journey to Italy the vessel in which he sailed was driven by stormy weather to shelter at Lulworth Cove. It was on board ship there that he wrote the following sonnet, one of the noblest in our language :

[1] See *Flame of Freedom:* the Story of the Tolpuddle Martyrs, by Owen Rattenbury (Epworth Press).

Bright star, would I were stedfast as thou art,
  Not in lone splendour hung aloft the night
And watching with eternal lids apart,
  Like nature's patient, sleepless Eremite,
The moving waters at their priestlike task
  Of cold ablution round earth's human shores,
Or gazing on the new soft-fallen mask
  Of snows upon the mountains and the moors—
No—yet still stedfast, still unchangeable,
  Pillow'd upon my fair love's ripening breast,
To feel for ever its soft fall and swell,
  Awake for ever in a sweet unrest,
Still, still to hear her tender taken breath,
  And so live ever—or else swoon to death.

The majestic cliffs of the Dorset coast from Ringstead Bay, near Poxwell, to the extreme point of Purbeck, are among the finest in the country. In stormy weather they are also among the most dangerous. Broken into bold headlands with coves and caverns below, and rock arches through which sea water runs at nearly all states of the tide, it is a stretch of coastland of exceptional interest. The lighthouses fixed at various points, the life-boat station at Kimmeridge, all indicate danger when storms rage in the Channel. Wrecks have inevitably taken place on such a coast at various periods of time, and men and women in sight of the land have taken their last breath, overwhelmed in a savage sea. A disaster occurred here in the eighteenth century when the East Indiaman *Halsewell* struck on the rocks and went down near Seacombe. Some hundred and fifty people were drowned, among them a number of young and accomplished women. The Rev. William Crowe, at that time apparently resident in Dorset as rector of Stoke Abbott, wrote a poem on the loss of the vessel. The *Halsewell* had left London in fair weather but was met off the Hampshire coast by a terrific Channel gale, and was 'swallowed up,' he wrote, 'by Neptune's wild and foamy jaws.'

The Rev. William Crowe was a man of culture, now forgotten by the rank and file like many another writer of musical verse. But the sequestered village of Stoke Abbott, lovely for situation, remembers his name and his fame though a century has gone since the tablet to his memory was placed on the wall of the church porch. Stoke Abbott lies in a deep hollow, in summer a veritable sleepy hollow, over which, however, the dawn of each new day spreads slowly like hands in blessing, and the enveloping shades of eventide come like a benediction. The tablet in the porch records that the poet Crowe was public orator in the university of Oxford, and that in his poem on Lewesdon Hill 'are garnered worthy thoughts—the fruit of frequent musings on that height.' Like Thomas Hardy in his poem 'Wessex Heights,' written nearly a century later, the Rev. William Crowe drew inspiration on and from Lewesdon Hill, one of the lesser Wessex Heights. Another poem of Crowe's on 'The Miseries of War' is a condemnation of the call to arms. It reminds one of the Cumberland poet's 'Invocation to the Earth' at the close of the Napoleonic wars of the same period. The majestic measure of the latter poem is but one of its several beauties. The Crowe poem is in blank verse.

The loss of the *Earl of Abergavenny*, also an East Indiaman, on the Chesil Beach near Weymouth, some twenty years after the wreck of the *Halsewell*, seems to have gone unsung by any Dorset poet. Captain Wordsworth, brother of the poet of that name, was commander of the *Abergavenny*, with which he went down. His body was recovered from the sea after one week's immersion and was buried at Wyke. To that tragedy we owe the poem to the daisy, beginning :

Sweet flower ! belike one day to have
A place upon thy poet's grave,
   I welcome thee once more.
But he, who was on land, at sea
My brother, too, in loving thee,
Although he loved more silently,
   Sleeps by his native shore.

The Hon. Mrs. Norton, Caroline Sheridan, a granddaughter of the dramatist, Richard Brinsley Sheridan, was a Dorset poet now much neglected and almost forgotten. Yet her address to the then Duchess of Sutherland, to whom her poetry was dedicated, is Byronic in expression and fire, as it is in tender feeling. Her marriage proved unhappy, and her poem to the Duchess is an expression of the sorrow which filled her heart mixed with scorn for that gnawing grief.

Once more, my harp ! once more, although I thought
   Never to wake thy silent strings again,

A wandering dream thy gentle chords have wrought,
And my sad heart, which long hath dwelt in pain,
Soars like a wild bird from a cypress bough,
Into the poet's heaven and leaves dull grief below!

The poem, one of many, proceeds with the same unhalting rhythm throughout, with simile and imagery both choice and beautiful. In another poem a picture is drawn of the death-bed of the great dramatist after the loss of his London theatre by fire, visited only by Samuel Rogers of all the great ones he had known. The home of the Sheridans was Frampton Court in Dorset in the upper reaches of the vale of Froom. Caroline Norton's 'Picture of Twilight,' in which she described the return of the labourer from his work as evening falls, was inspired by familiar Dorset scenes. There is a Spenserian touch in these beautiful descriptive lines. First she apostrophizes the fall of evening as follows, and then describes in detail the tired journey home:

O Twilight! Spirit that dost render birth
To dim enchantments; melting heaven with earth,
Leaving on craggy hills and running streams
A softness like the atmosphere of dreams;
Thy hour to all is welcome! Faint and sweet
Thy light falls round the peasant's homeward feet,
Who, slow returning from his task of toil,
Sees the low sunset gild the cultured soil,
And, though such radiance round him brightly glows,
Marks the small spark his cottage window throws.
Still as his heart forestalls his weary pace,
Fondly he dreams of each familiar face,
Recalls the treasures of his narrow life—

His rosy children and his sunburnt wife,
To whom his coming is the chief event
Of simple days in cheerful labour spent.
The rich man's chariot hath gone whirling past,
And these poor cottagers have only cast
One careless glance on all that show of pride,
Then to their tasks turned quietly aside ;
But him they wait for, him they welcome home ;
Fixed sentinels look forth to see him come ;
The fagot sent for when the fire grew dim,
The frugal meal prepared, are all for him ;
For him the watching of that sturdy boy,
For him those smiles of tenderness and joy,
For him—who plods his sauntering way along,
Whistling the fragment of some village song !

Of the out-of-doors poems of Thomas Hardy there are many charming for association as well as beauty of thought. Who that has climbed Pilsdon Pen and Inkpen Beacon, or seen Blackmoor Vale half full of tapering elms spread below 'homely' Bulbarrow, and lived for a space within sight of Wylls Neck, one of the loveliest of southern hills, but must read 'Wessex Heights' with keen relish as of the breathing of mountain air. In the poem the greater stress is laid on Ingpen Beacon and Wylls Neck in Somerset. These two hills are very dissimilar, neither is in Dorset, and each one is mentioned twice. Ingpen Beacon does not possess the beauty of Wylls Neck. It is one of the highest points of the chalk hills on the Wiltshire border, and from it in a past age beacon fires sent quick warning of danger far and wide over hill and valley. The beacon fire on Ingpen would throw its light to Reading, some twenty miles away, down the vale of Kennet. It is a lonely hill which should be climbed on foot. A small car may be driven within a mile of the summit. There are beech woods scattered about the Wiltshire hills as there are on the chalk lands of Dorset.

Wylls Neck is an arresting Quantock height, the highest point of the Somerset range. It is a hill of red sandstone rock and red earth, clothed in green in spring and summer, with feathery mantle of bracken in autumn turning to gold and brown. When there is play of white trailing mists up and over the steeply-sloping sides of this brightly-coloured hill, with beams of sunlight slashing in between, then it is singularly beautiful. The description of this eminence in 'Wessex Heights,' as a hill 'for thinking, dreaming, dying on,' reveals the fact that the colours and contours of Wylls Neck had strongly appealed to the poet's artistic sense. It is twice mentioned in the poem, both times following Ingpen Beacon, as if second thoughts were best.

The ballad-tragedy of gipsy passions in Somerset 'where Dunkery frowns on Exon Moor' makes pleasant reading as one conjures up afresh the scenery of that wild country. From the desolate moor above Oare and the Lorna Doone guest-house located in a deep hollow beyond Dunkery, to Marlbury Downs and back again over the Mendips, seems a likely circuit for the gilted vans from which handsome gipsy women peep out as they pass along the roads. Marlbury Downs, mentioned in the poem, must indicate the wide-spreading chalk hills around Marlborough and Inkpen in Wiltshire. The gipsies, like the vagrants of Wessex, probably made a regular journey round the district, turning up at the same place again after the lapse of only a few months. The older women of this class suffer badly from varicose veins. If quietly told at your door that they called some months ago for alms, they reply, 'No, dearie, you have never seen me before.'

In the swift action of the Exmoor ballad there is no leisure for the 'thinker of crooked thoughts' to cogitate on the affairs of men and their fate. Wrong doing with retribution following fast in its wake is over and done with before the end of the poem and Dunkery, one of 'the everlasting hills,' goes on frowning as before. One bowed figure is left on the moor in the throes of human compassion.

But 'The Abbey Mason' which follows the ballad in the *Collected Poems of Thomas Hardy* agitates the mind so thoroughly that 'crooked thoughts' well up like a muddy fountain that will not be reduced to quiescence. A darksome mist gathers about Gothic pinnacle and tower, and the heavens laugh in scorn at man's most laudable efforts, while the gods descend to steal away his fire. If retribution swiftly follows the evil doer, punishment just as heavy falls on the head of those who excel in capacity or goodness. The poem, it may be was founded on a legend which intentionally illustrates the truth.

The savage storm which ushered in 'the homecoming' of the young bride to some cottage on Toller Down is aptly described in the refrain of the poem under that title.

> Gruffly growled the wind on Toller downland
> bleak and bare.

On the great broad back of the haunted down much happened it may be, in the days of long ago. Near Toller Down Gate are huge stones which, it is said, have seen exciting history. But whether the uncanny psychology of the down points to long past human sacrifices accompanied by druidical rites, or its stern admonitory power escapes from disembodied remembrance of innocent men, gibbeted by the highway, one cannot tell. Toller Down is exposed to every wind that blows. It was on a spur of this great down that Shepherd Oak played the flute in the dead of night. And it was here that Thomas Hardy noted the changing colours of Aldebaran and Betelgeux, two prominent stars in the constellation Orion.

CHAPTER XIII

'THE SLANTEN LIGHT O' FALL'

AN English speaking poet pondering over the magnificence of American woodlands in autumn, exclaimed, ' O what a glory doth this world put on.' It is to this, the artistic side of the human temperament that the beauty of autumn appeals. We do not consider that in this wonderful autumnal pageant Nature has set out on her annual economic campaign. Why should we ? Is not beauty, of itself, enough ? Yet, stay. All through the long light days of summer the leaves, now so beautiful in tints of red, yellow, gold and brown, have caught the sunlight and stored it up for use in winter and in spring. Their work done, they lose their freshness and instead of making quiet, rustling music on the passing breeze, a faint crisp rattling, almost uncanny through hours of darkness, tells that the Fall is near. Complex chemical changes have taken place, and everything that can be of use in the general economy is sent back into stem or twig before the leaf falls. A layer of corklike matter formed at the base of the leaf-stalk shuts out the leaf from intercourse with the tree. It is while these changes are taking place that the green of the leaf is changed for yellow, red or brown. The tints depend upon the character and proportion of acids present within the leaf.

It is popularly supposed that the trees of one species exhibit everywhere the same colours when fading. That, however, is only true within limits. The leaves of the chestnut tree in one district may fade in tints of lemon and yellow, and in another a deep red colour may prevail. The leaves of the rowan are said by observers to turn brown or scarlet, while some I have seen in the north country are dyed a brilliant crimson. Birches change their green for a delicate yellow, an exquisite tint when contrasted with the black and silver bark of the trunks, and the crimson of the rowan—a combination of colouring few artists could correctly capture:

> Bright yellow, red and orange,
> The leaves come down in hosts,
> Once they were Indian Princes,
> But now they're changed to Ghosts.

In late October elm trees still wear their robes of green, but a few nights of frost will work a transformation. Already other trees, such as the age-old poplars down by the placid river, and here and there an ash tree half tilted on the brink, have felt the frosty chill of winter approaching in the night, though the days be warm and sunny. A crisp yellow carpet spread widely out in a circle beneath the stately poplars tells that the season of the Fall is with us. It is interesting to note that yellow is the colour to which English poets give most prominence in their poetry on autumn.

They speak of 'yellowing woods' or the 'yellowing hand' of autumn. The father of American poetry, accustomed to the magnificence of changing maple woods wrote of the 'coloured landscape' which, together with his phrase of 'painted leaves,' suggests other colours than yellow and green. The autumn woods, he says, 'have put their glory on,' a telling expression which had influenced Longfellow, unconsciously, when he exclaimed, 'Oh, what a glory doth this world put on.'

The Dorset hedgerows of field maple, hawthorn and dogwood are rich in shades of red and yellow, scarlet, crimson and purple, and the glamour of autumn spreads over every berry-bearing herb and shrub. Luscious-looking bryony berries festoon neglected hedgerows in all the varying shades from pale ivory to rich scarlet. Spikes of privet berries, pyramidal in shape, ten to twenty berries in a spike, crowd the roadside hedges with black, tempting fruits. In thickets and along numberless hedgerows of remoter places, berries of the helio-flowered iris shine within their bursting capsules like strings of coral gems.

When the trees and hedges begin to flame with autumnal tints, the half-sweet, half-acrid smell of decaying vegetation lies heavy on the air. Nothing seems to dissipate this acridity of the atmosphere until the first night frost drifts hither from the east, or the first gale of the Fall comes blowing up the Channel. The autumn pungency of the air is thickest by the river where the deep stream makes a graceful curve round an acre of level, soppy woodland crowded with undergrowth.

Great horsetail, yellow tansy, hemp agrimony and willowherb replete with feathery plumes, quaint monkshood most acrid of all, contrive to produce a pungent smell in decay. The essence of every plant, apparently, has been extracted on the spot. The dell lies at the foot of a scarp from which at some past time a tract of ground may have slipped down, for legend tells of a happy island here. But there is no island in the still, deep river. The boughs of ash, elm and poplar mirrored in the still water, almost touch the broad-leaved, low-growing alders on the opposite bank of the river. The bough of an ash-tree which overhangs the river provides an accommodating lookout for a blue kingfisher. From where I stand I can see the long beak and ruddy breast. Even as I look the bird makes a lightning plunge downward to secure a tasty meal and disappears one knows not where. Tomtits and greattits in the pine trees at the top of the scarp flit about and call to each other in silver notes. All through one's half-hour watch of the play of golden leaves coming crisply down from the trees, the accompaniment of silvern sounds falls from the needle-leaved pine trees.

Anon a gorgeous blue streak flashes through the dell between the trunks of the trees swift and straight as an arrow, going down stream. It is the kingfisher again making for the willows, where dainty grey-yellow warblers rear fresh young broods each summer. Long yellow leaves from willows higher up the river come floating down on the placid water. Crimson foliage of the red-berried guelder catches against the bank under a tuft of 'bowen zedge,' as the Dorset writer of rural verse calls the graceful carex pendula. A puff of wind high up in the trees brings down the yellow poplar leaves in a cloud, when, suddenly, a creature of brilliant blue flashes by upstream between the trunks of the trees, followed instantly by another. The sun is going down, and the kingfishers are off to the protecting tunnel in the river bank or scarp, neighbours, perhaps, of the bats which in late afternoon fly over the tallest poplars.

The pageant of autumn is not at an end even in November when the great elms of the avenue and of Blackmoor Vale are clothed in orange and yellow, and hedgerows are patched with crimson and gold. The glorious colour of elm trees often persists until the end of the month, the leaves slowly yellowing and falling like the leaves of oak.

The beech trees of Toller and Bubb Downs, before late November, have lost much of the burning aspect which makes so gorgeous a display in October. The fascination of flaming beech trees in sunlight—of the red smouldering carpet spread thickly over the floor of the woodland—of the long strips of burning leaves which edge the open road for many miles in different parts of the county—comes as a new experience each autumn. Lemon, orange, russet, copper, and every shade of brown cover the numerous wood-lands of beech upon the chalk and the downlands. For a moment one feels tempted to describe the display as Nature's colourful swansong. But such an analogy would be false as well as sentimental. Nature does not die on so grand a scale.

The beech woods on Bubb Down, more especially, perhaps, than many others, catch 'the slanten light o' fall.' The side of the down on which the the mile-long woods occur slopes sharply to the west, and the October sun, slanting to its setting, shines with amber light on the wood floor of burning leaves and upon the straight, grey trunks of beech. The wood floor and the grey trunks, thus lighted by the sun, throw an added glow of sunlight upwards to the yellow leaves remaining on the trees. A woodland palace of sylvan gold is the immediate and exquisite result. To walk within it is to dream for a space in a fabulous realm of gold.

The poet Tennyson wrote:

> A spirit haunts the year's last hours,
> Dwelling amid these yellowing bowers:
> To himself he talks.

Southey, reflecting on autumn, spoke of the rich variety of hues which,

> Make yonder forest in the slanting sun
> So beautiful.

The same idea was rendered by the Rev. W. Barnes, all unconscious of Southey, into 'The Slanten Light o' Fall'—a beautiful climax of expression.

Among the crisp, brown leaves which carpet the wood floor on Melbury Bubb in autumn, pheasants search for food, probably for the angular nuts of the beech. There are many beech woods of various size scattered about the slopes of the downs between Beaminster, Hooke Park and Maiden Newton as well as on the higher hills, such as Bubb Down, Revel Hill and High Stoy. Some one of these woods is indicated in the journey of Tess from the farm where she served beyond the river Brit, to her post at Flintcombe Ash. The night's vigil in the wood, where pheasants which had been maimed by sportsmen fell from the boughs at intervals through the night, will readily be recalled, together with the girl's melancholy reflections thereon when day came to throw light upon the scene.

The beech wood on Bubb Down, like many another wood in Dorset is frequented by the cheerful, and quaintly named nuthatch. The nuthatch is a busy, lovable bird, careless of observation. It runs quickly up and down the trunks of trees and round the branches just as a tree-creeper will, but its movements are quicker and neater than a creeper's, which must rely partly on its tail for support. The slaty grey back and buff underparts of the nuthatch, with flanks and breast of a rich chestnut colour, render it an inconspicuous bird in autumn. It haunts old parklands where trees are often covered with grey and green-grey lichens. In spring and summer its cheerful voice is often heard in Dorset as in Devon, though it is not often seen in the umbrageous shade of beech and elm. I have watched its progress up to fifty or sixty feet along the branches of graceful old elm trees, its neat figure silhouetted against the sky on some slender twig thickly fringed with lichens. I have seen it tapping with its strong beak on a bough a dozen feet above my head, its bright eyes showing no sign of fear though aware of my close attention. The call note is clear, strong and musical, and might be interpreted as 'poick, poick.' It has none of the hardness of the chaffinch's 'pink, pink,' which resounds perennially in the beech woods of the south.

The movements of all birds are circumscribed in summer when occupied with nesting affairs. With autumn comes liberty, and flocks of some kinds travel far and wide. In the autumn of 1930 I watched a flock of starlings, some five or six hundred strong, every day as afternoon melted into evening flying southeast at a good height. The birds came from the direction of the higher hills, Lewesdon and Pilsdon Pen. At first the flight was seen about six o'clock, then a little earlier each week as the days grew shorter. The rendezvous for the night was a pleasant woodland not far from the sea near Puncknowle, some ten miles from the place where the flock appeared first to take the air. These huge gatherings are, no doubt, composed of northern birds which have come to winter in the south. They feed in pastures and on ploughlands where the soil is usually turned over in autumn.

Berries of all kinds are eaten by birds, and starlings take toll of elder-berries in early autumn. A long hedgerow of berry-laden elders may be seen bending low under the heavy birds. In an endeavour to gratify a taste for the purple fruit, they swing in the air with wings outspread while clawing on to the long, swaying branches.

Elder-berries disappear from the hedgerows long before the more bitter privet berries. Some of the latter may still be found in winter when ivy-berries are ripening and changing from green to black. In a fruit-laden hawthorn bush a hen blackbird will perch among the small branches and eat a score of berries at a meal. From one twig after another she will pick off the ripest and softest of the berries. Blackbird and thrush every autumn and winter nullify commendable efforts to keep gardens bright with berries. The thrush, with beautiful spotted breast will sit upon a daphne bush eating your scarlet berries while you stand near watching the theft. The hen blackbird, who is of a sooty brown colour, will steal berberis berries, a dozen or so at a time, flying off with a chuckle when reproved. Blackbirds are very common in Dorset in every valley, by every stream. A family of four reared in a boss of ivy within my garden in the summer of 1931 consisted of three brown hen birds and one pied blackbird, the latter being evenly marked with white on wings, neck, and head. In early autumn the pied bird secured a mate with sandy breast, suggestive in its light colour of the hen bird of the ring-ousel.

When the voice of the song-thrush is hushed in the autumn, then the wren may be heard piping forth at dawn. The vociferous engaging song is known to all who dwell in the country. The neat little figure with the perky tail silhouetted against the sky outside one's window as it runs up or down the walls, indicates that spiders which lurk in corners are in demand for breakfast. The little bird will assiduously search each corner of the window frame if not alarmed by movements indoors.

Quite as industrious, and small almost as the wren, is the pretty coletit, which one may often see on an early morning walk carefully examining roadside banks or garden where seed may perchance be found. The whitish-grey mark reaching from head to nape distinguishes this species from the marshtit. The latter is a beautiful bird with black cap reaching down to the eyes. I have seen birds of this species seeking food with coletits among grass under elm and beech. The buff or ruddy colour of the marshtit on breast and flanks is occasionally so bright as to vie with the pink of the longtailed species of titmouse.

Every morning in autumn one may see rooks passing overhead towards the sea where they feed in quiet places on the beach. The poet Crabbe mentions this habit in his sketch on autumn and remarks on the return of the birds by the same route at night. That was over a hundred years ago. Habits in Nature alter but little. The daily visit to the sea is as prevalent now as it was in the time of Crabbe. One thing the poet does not mention which is perhaps of comparatively rare occurrence. I have heard an old rook on an autumn afternoon when returning from the sea, crooning softly to itself in the homeward flight.

What could such crooning mean but contentment in anticipation of reaching home again.

There is an abstract idea, a parable, if you will in that beautiful phrase, 'The Slanten Light o' Fall,' running parallel in the mind with the natural phenomena of autumn. A poet has declared that:

> In youth we love the darksome lawn
>   Brushed by the owlet's wing;
> Then, twilight is preferred to dawn,
>   And autumn to the spring.

Yet most journals, in the nature of things do testify in spring to the presence of the spring poet who is usually very young. But not more than once in a century does the output include anything so virile as daffodils 'tossing their heads in sprightly dance,' or so jubilant as the thrush trying to 'recapture, that first, fine careless rapture.'

And what youthful autumn poet ever rose to the dignity of expression of the seventy-third Shakespearian sonnet!

> That time of year thou may'st in me behold
>   When yellow leaves, or none, or few, do hang
> Upon those boughs which shake against the cold,
>   Bare ruin's choirs, where late the sweet birds sang.
> In me thou see'st the twilight of such day
>   As after sunset fadeth in the west,
> Which by and by black night doth take away,
>   Death's second self, that seals up all in rest.

Both the measure and the words of the sonnet are without fire, emotion or regret. A smooth calm born of experience pervades the lines and gives them the strength, not only of beauty, but of a rhythmic onward movement—an effortless carrying forward on the breast of Time, as it were. The personal element is the essence of the Shakespeare sonnet, though the pronoun rarely occurs, and the picture which at first is purely autumnal fades away into 'The Slanten Light o' Fall.'

'Quiet coves his soul has in its autumn, when his wings he furleth close,' wrote the youthful poet who sleeps at Rome—the youthful poet who stands almost alone in the realm of literature with his address to autumn, a poem containing thirty-three lines of beautiful imagery and nature lore. Without hinting even remotely at any parallelism between autumn and the later years of human life, John Keats contrived with great spirit to paint a swift picture of the bounty of 'the season of mists,' so swift indeed that pensive melancholy had no time to lift her head.

> Let me enjoy the earth no less
> Because the all-enacting Might
> That fashioned forth its loveliness
> Had other aims than my delight,

wrote Thomas Hardy, the tried friend of the Dorset dialect poet who wrote so sweetly of 'The Slanten Light o' Fall.'

BIBLIOGRAPHIA

The Story of Forde Abbey – – Heath.

Earthworks of Cranbourne Chase – Heywood Sumner.

Parish of Ashmore – – – Watson.

The Roman Era in Britain – – John Ward.

A Key to Domesday – – – R W. Eyton.